THROW LIKE A GIRL, CHEER LIKE A BOY

THROW LIKE A GIRL,
CHEER LIKE A BOY

The Evolution of Gender, Identity, and Race in Sports

Robyn Ryle

ROWMAN & LITTLEFIELD
Lanham • Boulder • New York • London

Published by Rowman & Littlefield
An imprint of The Rowman & Littlefield Publishing Group, Inc.
4501 Forbes Boulevard, Suite 200, Lanham, Maryland 20706
www.rowman.com

6 Tinworth Street, London SE11 5AL

British Library Cataloguing in Publication Information Available

Library of Congress Cataloging-in-Publication Data

Names: Ryle, Robyn, author.
Title: Throw like a girl, cheer like a boy : the evolution of gender, identity, and race in sports / Robyn
   Ryle.
Description: Lanham, Maryland : Rowman & Littlefield, 2020. | Includes bibliographical references
   and index. | Summary: "This book looks at the intersection of sports and identities, using sports
   to reveal the complicated history of gender, sexuality, race, and social justice while connecting
   those stories to the world of today's athletes. It highlights the ways sports often contribute to
   inequalities, but also how they can help make the world more accepting"— Provided by publish-
   er.
Identifiers: LCCN 2019040034 (print) | LCCN 2019040035 (ebook) | ISBN 9781538130667 (cloth) |
   ISBN 9781538130674 (epub)
Subjects: LCSH: Sports—Sex differences. | Racism in sports. | Discrimination in sports. | Sex dis-
   crimination in sports. | Homophobia in sports.
Classification: LCC GV706.5 .R95 2020 (print) | LCC GV706.5 (ebook) | DDC 306.4/83—dc23
LC record available at https://lccn.loc.gov/2019040034
LC ebook record available at https://lccn.loc.gov/2019040035

CONTENTS

ACKNOWLEDGMENTS

Thanks to Amelia Appel for her enthusiasm and persistence with this book, as well as Brent Taylor and all the other amazing folks at Triada US. So proud to be part of their team. Thank you to Christen Karniski, Jessica McCleary, Erinn Slanina, and everyone at Rowman & Littlefield for giving this book a home.

Part of my love for sports came from my parents, who are enthusiastic fans and participants. They were happy to cheer me and my siblings on in whatever sport we took up, as well as making possible marathon games of badminton in our backyard.

A marriage to someone who was completely uninterested in sports might have worked for me, but I doubt it. Luckily I found a person who was not only very interested in sports, but interested in the same ways. Jeff can always tell you how many managers of color there are in Major League Baseball in any given season, and will enthusiastically take up the argument for why women's sports are just as good as men's. His encyclopedic knowledge of sports and his excellent editing skills also come in handy. This book wouldn't have happened without our countless conversations.

Finally, thank you to all the athletes and activists who continue to inspire me and make sports better for all of us.

INTRODUCTION

I love sports. I love playing sports, whether it was tennis in high school or intramural flag football as a graduate student. I love watching sports, especially football and baseball and soccer. I love thinking about sports from a sociological perspective, which means asking a lot of questions about why sports are the way they are, as well as paying attention to the relationship between sport and inequality. Most of all, I love talking about sports. If there's a way to bring up sports in the college classrooms where I teach, I'll find it. About half of the conversations my partner and I have on a daily basis are about sports, which might sound insane, but is actually true.

I wrote this book because I love sports in all those ways. I love sports in the best sense of what it means to love something, which is to say, not blindly or uncritically. I love sports even though I believe they could be better. I'm there even through the flaws and the imperfections. I'm always rooting, not just for my favorite teams, but for sports to become a fairer and more just world. That's part of what this book is about—the quest for a better sports world.

This book is also a journey into the ways sports can teach us a lot about the wider world. The transition in cheerleading from all men to almost all women teaches us important lessons about gender segregation, not just in sports, but in the workplace as well. The history of gender testing in sports reveals the flaws in many of our everyday assumptions about what gender is. Asking questions about the differences between women and men's athletic abilities challenges our ideas about what we mean when we talk about gender differences in the first place, as well as why we're so obsessed with proving who is better or worse at one thing or another. When we consider how to include transgender athletes into sports, we are forced to question what the very purpose of playing should be. Looking at sexuality in sport leads to an interrogation of the connections between gender and sexuality that exist in larger society. Sports can also serve as a mirror of the history of how power has been distributed on a global level and how categories of race and ethnicity have been created and then changed over time. Finally, sports activists can provide role models for making our world more equal and just. There is a lot to learn from sports if you ask the right questions, and that's what we will be doing in this book.

This book is for fans of all kinds of different sports, from cheerleading to soccer to polo to cricket to figure skating. It's also for people who are only mildly interested in sports, but want to know more about the history of gender, sexuality, and race as seen through a unique lens. In this book, you'll learn a little bit of sociology and a lot about sports through a historical and cross-cultural perspective. There is so much more to say about the connections between sport, gender, race, and sexuality than can be contained within these pages, so hopefully, this will serve as an introduction to this fascinating world.

Sports can make us laugh and cry. They bring us together to cheer on a team. Sometimes they pull us apart, divided over who gets to play and how and whether they should be able to use their athletic platform to push for social change. Sports give us joy, and it is out of my own joy of sports that this book emerges. I hope this book broadens that joy for readers with a deeper knowledge of where sport has been and the hopeful directions in which it might go.

I

WHEN ALL CHEERLEADERS WERE BOYS

Sports and Gender Segregation

In 1911, a prominent magazine proclaimed that "the reputation of having been a valiant 'cheer-leader' is one of the most valuable things a boy can take away from college. As a title to promotion in professional or public life, it ranks hardly second to that of having been a quarter-back."[1] As the quotation implies, being a cheerleader in college set young men on the path to success once they graduated and moved on to the rest of their lives. Early cheerleaders were often also the captains of other sports teams, and were seen as heroic figures in the masculine world of sports and competition. Cheerleaders were hand-picked by committees of faculty, physical education departments, and student body groups. To be a cheerleader was to be a shining example of leadership and athleticism, an honor for college men. Cheerleaders were the ultimate model of masculinity—the kind of men all the other guys wanted to be.

Today 97 percent of all cheerleaders are women, and boys who cheer are hardly ever seen as manly.[2] So what happened? Why did cheerleading experience a total gender reversal?

ROOTER KINGS, YELL LEADERS, AND THE BIRTH OF CHEERLEADING

To understand the strange history of gender in cheerleading, we have to go back to the very beginning, to the story of when cheerleading first began. The University of Pennsylvania claims to have organized the first-ever cheer ensemble in 1894, though the Princeton Yell, a pep club, had already been around for a decade. These groups of men were sometimes called "rooter kings" or "yell leaders" and they became a crucial part of the college football scene. Cheerleading was important enough to have its own national fraternity—Gamma Sigma—and every year they partnered with sports journalists to pick an All-American cheer squad, the best of the best in the cheerleading world.[3]

The skills associated with being a male cheerleader weren't that different from what we expect from cheerleaders today. They yelled and led the crowd in cheers. They had megaphones, which they often tossed around. They would arch their body from side to side and shake their fists at the crowd as they encouraged them to enthusiastically root for their team. These early cheerleaders wore full-length white trousers with a V-neck sweater and a hat, very different from the short skirts we've come to expect today. Male cheerleaders were so important to college football games that they sometimes got blamed when the team lost. As cheerleading evolved, it came to incorporate some of the more athletic aspects that we associate with cheerleading today. Squads began to include gymnastics, like at the University of Kentucky, where boys wishing to try out had to first complete a six-week tumbling course.

HOG-CALLERITIS AND WHY WOMEN MAKE LOUSY CHEERLEADERS

It wasn't until the 1930s that some women began to show up on cheerleading squads. When women did start cheering, their presence was often met with hostility. They still weren't eligible for election to the All-American squad, and some universities, like the University of Pittsburgh, outright banned girls from cheerleading. The University of Pittsburgh didn't lift their ban on women as cheerleaders until 1954.[4]

The arguments against women as cheerleaders at places like the University of Pittsburgh rested on two assumptions: that women lacked the necessary skills to be cheerleaders, and that participating in cheerleading would make girls "too masculine for their own good."[5] Experts of the time argued that girls clearly couldn't perform the gymnastic stunts required to be on a squad. Women and girls weren't athletic enough to go flipping through the air like the men and boys. Additionally, all the yelling required of cheerleaders would lead to "hog-calleritis," or "loud, raucous voices" that were clearly not appropriate for young ladies. It was also argued that cheerleading would cause girls to become "overly conceited."[6] In sum, cheerleading was too hard for women, in addition to running the risk of making them too full of themselves and giving them voices that sounded too much like men.

PLAY DAYS, TEA, AND EARLY WOMEN'S SPORTS

Girls in this time period weren't leading cheers, but they still played sports, even if the sports they were playing were different from those of boys. For middle-class and upper-class women, physical education programs began at colleges and universities as early as the 1860s and 1870s. These programs were governed solely by women and gave college women an opportunity to participate in at least 14 different sports, with basketball being especially popular. Beyond college campuses, many working-class women bowled and played softball and basketball for industrial leagues, usually sponsored by companies or factories. At many high schools—especially small, rural schools that lacked enough students for intramural play or substituted competitive sports for physical education—women's basketball thrived.[7]

As far back as the late nineteenth and early twentieth centuries, women were playing sports, but the idea of women athletes made some people nervous. Women who led physical education programs worked to ensure that the sports girls played never became too competitive, due to concerns that competition would lead to strenuous physical activity that might harm women's menstrual cycles, their ability to have children, and their attractiveness to potential spouses. The fear was that if girls got too competitive on the basketball court, they might not be able to get married or become mothers, and these were seen as two central roles for women to fulfill.[8]

This fear of competitiveness meant that girls could play basketball, but not the same version of basketball that boys played. Not long after basketball was invented in 1891, female physical education professionals came up with a modified version of the game that would be safe and appropriate for girls. Girls' basketball had six players rather than five, with three offensive and three defensive players on each team. Girls couldn't cross the half-court line because it would cause too much exertion, and could only dribble three times before they had to pass the ball. In girls' basketball, players were forbidden from doing anything as masculine as snatching the ball from their opponents. Not surprisingly, these rules made girls' basketball a slower game to watch as well as to play.[9]

Those in charge of women's sports were also concerned that too much competition would cause women emotional distress, sending them into a state of hysterics. Or that the women might get scratched up in a way that would lead to blemishes on their faces, which would destroy their "feminine charms."[10] The question of who would watch women play sports also posed potential problems. Would men be allowed as spectators? What would women wear while they played, and how would they ensure their bodies were properly covered? How could women be protected from the hundreds of potentially leering eyes?

Because of these fears, women's sports at the collegiate level remained a deeply segregated and secluded institution. From the top to the bottom, women's sports were played and controlled by women who worked hard to protect female athletes from the dangers of too much competition, as well as what they saw as the commercialism and exploitation rampant in men's sports. In men's sports, the health and well-being of all athletes were sacrificed to the irresistible urge to win at all costs. Men's sports produced stars, but they didn't provide equal opportunities for all men to participate in physical education, which was an important goal for women's sports participation.

Women's physical education defined itself against the corrupt world of men's sports, and that meant downplaying the competitive part of sports as much as possible. Instead of tournaments, women would often have "play days." On play days, teams from other schools would come and visit—but rather than competing against each other, women from different schools would be distributed evenly across teams. The only way to tell who was from which schools were the colored pinnies (pinafores) or aprons they wore. All the women would share a locker room to encourage sociability and, at the end of the day, they might all have tea or a meal together before heading back to their home schools. Play days emphasized the participation of *all* over the elite performance of a *few* that characterized men's sports.[11]

Some historically black colleges and universities (HBCUs) did depart from this noncompetitive model. This was because they were sheltered from or ignored by the dominant model of physical education programs at white colleges. That HBCUs decided to go their own way allowed them to develop some of the most successful women's athletic programs of the time period. At Tennessee State University, the Tigerbelles developed a premier track and field program for their women athletes, winning the Amateur Athletic Union (AAU) competition every year from 1956 through 1968. Women from Tennessee State accounted for 25 of the 40 Olympic medals won by women in track and field between 1948 and 1968.[12]

WORLD WAR II AND THE BIG SWITCH

During the time period when all cheerleaders were male, most women were playing their own sports, even if many of them weren't allowed to get too competitive. At the same time, there were concerns that if girls started cheerleading, they would become manly and conceited. So what changed? The simple answer is that World War II brought about a rapid transformation in cheerleading. As it did for many areas of social life, World War II altered the relationship between gender and sports, and this wasn't only because women flooded into cheerleading to take the place of men fighting overseas, though this did happen in some places.

During the war, colleges scaled back on *all* extracurricular activities that weren't seen as essential, which included sports programs for women. A 1943 survey found that most colleges had either eliminated or reduced their women's sports programs. As a result, some women became cheerleaders to fill the gap left by men fighting overseas.[13] But women were also looking for a physical activity to take the place of their disappearing sports programs.[14] Cheerleading became a convenient way for women accustomed to being physically active to maintain that life-style.

With increasing numbers of women leading the cheers from the side-lines, the meaning of cheerleading changed. Cheerleading couldn't be considered an inherently masculine activity anymore if it was being done mostly by women. It also wouldn't be seen as a first step in a successful and ambitious career beyond college, as it had been for men. Cheerleading became viewed as a much less important activity when women filled its ranks. When women led cheers, it wasn't a reflection of their leadership skills and athleticism. In fact, much of the athleticism that had been associated with cheerleading disappeared. Instead, cheerleading was increasingly sexualized. Descriptions of cheerleaders emphasized their appearance and attractiveness rather than their voice or ability to perform stunts. Cheerleaders were pretty and sexy, not future leaders and captains of industry.[15]

Outside the sporting world, the gender switch in cheerleading mirrors what happened in many occupational fields. The occupation we now call "secretary" used to be done by "clerks," who were all men. Clerks were certainly not expected to be cheerful and attractive, like proxy wives in an office setting. But when women began doing the same tasks clerks had once done, the job of secretary emphasized these feminine qualities. When most teachers in the United States were men, their authority and knowledge were seen as important qualities of the job. As women took over, nurturing and compassion became important characteristics for teaching.

It only took a couple of decades for cheerleading to completely switch into an activity seen as overwhelmingly and inarguably feminine. By the 1950s, cheerleading was no longer a prestigious, masculine domain. For a young woman, becoming a cheerleader was a surefire way to demonstrate the ideal form of femininity—pretty, nonathletic, and largely an accessory to men's activities.

BOYS OVER HERE AND GIRLS OVER THERE

The history of cheerleading may be unique in the world of sports in terms of the speed in which an activity achieved a complete and total reversal of gender expectations. It's hard to find another sport that has gone from being considered as manly as the football quarterback to about as girly as it gets in just a few decades. Ironically, today's cheerleading resembles the original version of the activity, even if it's mostly women who are involved. In some places, cheerleading has become a very competitive and athletically demanding sport. It is also one of the few sporting activities in which women and men compete together on a team.

We live in a world where most sports are gender-segregated, the number of sports that aren't can be counted on one hand. Sports where women and men do compete together include NASCAR racing, thoroughbred horse racing, equestrian events, and mixed doubles tennis. Across the rest of the sports world, organizations patrol a hard line between women and men. This line can be especially harmful to transgender and intersex athletes, topics which we'll explore more in chapters 2 and 4.

Even with the increasing numbers of openly transgender athletes, the gender segregation of sports remains a largely taken-for-granted fact of life. Before the women's movement in places like the United States, many men and women moved through a world that was highly gender-segregated across social spheres, so the gender separation we see in sports today didn't seem strange. But if you take a moment to think about how deeply gender-integrated most areas of our lives are today, you might wonder, what's so special about sports? Women and men go to school together and work together across almost all professions. They work out together in gyms and belong to many of the same clubs and organizations. There are very few areas of social life that remain gender-segregated. So why do we still insist that we can't step onto the field or the court together in a way not organized by gender?

There are some specific situations in which women and men play sports together. Many colleges and universities have co-ed intramural leagues. In some community leagues, women and men may play together. What these situations have in common is that the main purpose of playing is recreational. That isn't to say that some intramural games on college campuses don't get competitive, but in theory, people are playing just for the fun of it. When nothing serious is at stake, it's okay for girls and boys or women and men to play together.

Even in these gender-integrated situations, rules are put in place to make sure that gender-integrated sports remain "fair," and those rules are based on incorrect assumptions about gender. For example, in a co-ed basketball league, rules will probably require that at least two women be on the court at all times. The underlying assumption is that a team with four men and one woman would have an unfair advantage, because the men would be better athletes. We'll talk about prevailing assumptions regarding gender and athletic performance in chapter 3, but for now, it's fairly easy to see that although *some* men may be better basketball players than *some* women, there are also quite a few women who are better basketball players than some men. For example, a top player from the Women's National Basketball Association (WNBA) would easily be able to beat an average amateur male basketball player. If you had two WNBA players on your team, you'd probably have an unfair advantage over most teams made up of five amateur men. These specific rules about what gender-integrated sports look like make sense only if you assume that every single man is a better athlete than every single woman, and that's simply not the case.

THE COLD WAR AND WOMEN'S COMPETITION

The idea that competition was bad for women in sports began to change after World War II, and that happened in part because of the Cold War. This sustained political hostility that existed between the United States and the Soviet Union throughout the second half of the twentieth century created increased competition at many levels around the globe. Which country could boast the greatest economic prosperity? Which country could get to the moon first? Which country could win the most medals at the Olympic Games? This last competition dictated that women in the United States step up their sports game. The previous era, with its emphasis on cooperative play days, gradually disappeared in favor of programs that could produce elite female athletes—athletes who could show the Soviet Union and other Communist countries the inherent superiority of American democracy. Women's sports became more competitive in order to help the United States win the Cold War by accumulating as many Olympic medals as possible.[16]

In the same time period, women also started participating in a small number of professional sports. The Ladies Professional Golf Association (LPGA) was founded in 1950, making it the oldest women's professional sports league still in existence.[17] Made famous by the movie, *A League of Their Own*, the All-American Girls Professional Baseball League was created in 1943. The league was meant to fill the void in the baseball world left by the many men who were serving overseas. The league lasted until 1954, when a lack of audience and financial struggles forced the AAGPBL to shut down.[18]

Women would play golf and baseball professionally in a gender-segregated environment, but in the world of Formula One motorsports, women raced alongside men. Maria Teresa de Fillipis competed in Formula One racing in 1958–1959.[19] In the National Association of Stock Car Auto Racing (NASCAR), Sara Christian finished 14th out of 33 drivers in the NASCAR's first strictly stock car race in June 1949.[20] Lula Olive Gill and Ada Evans were riding horses and winning races right beside men early in the twentieth century in thoroughbred racing, and their successes came long before Kathy Kusner became the first licensed jockey in 1969.[21] These sports demonstrate that it is possible for women and men to play together and compete against each other in the same sport.

HALF-COURT BASKETBALL AND THE 37 WORDS THAT CHANGED THE WORLD

When Title IX of the Education Amendments of 1972 was passed, no one involved had sports on their mind. U.S. Senator from Indiana Birch Bayh, who helped win passage of the amendment, was asked during Senate hearings if Title IX would mean that women and men would share dormitories or other facilities on college campuses. Bayh assured his fellow senators that this would not be the case, and that the bill would not involve the desegregation of football fields or locker rooms. Senator Peter Dominick of Colorado responded with a joke that if football were gender-integrated when he was an undergraduate, he would have had a lot more fun playing. Despite the radical way Title IX ended up transforming sports, that brief exchange was the extent of any conversations about the implications Title IX might have for athletics before the bill was passed.[22]

That snippet of question and answer from the Senate hearing demonstrates the attitude women were up against during this time period. Senator Dominick's joke clearly implies that the only good reason to have women on a sports team would be their entertainment value for men. It also suggests that the idea to gender-integrate football teams wasn't completely outside the realm of possibility, even if it would take another 26 years before that vision came true. It wasn't until 1997 that a woman played on a college football team (Liz Heaston kicked for Willamette University, and is believed to be the first woman to ever score points in a college football game).[23] But Title IX would completely transform the terrain of sports in the United States by opening up new opportunities for women and girls. Before the passage of Title IX, there were 313,000 girls and women playing college and high school sports in the United States. Forty years later, there were over 3 million women and girls in the fields and on the courts.[24]

The fascinating truth about Title IX is that it very much slipped through the cracks as a piece of legislation, with many of those involved completely oblivious to its potential effects. Patsy Mink was one of the principal authors of Title IX. Mink was a Japanese American woman who represented Hawaii in the House of Representatives. She had experienced gender discrimination in the sports world as well as in the larger arena of education addressed by Title IX. These experiences shaped her commitment to gender and racial equality. She played basketball for Maui High School, but her team was never allowed to play full court because that much running would be too arduous for girls, consistent with notions that overexertion was dangerous for women. Mink was rejected from medical school 12 times due to what she believed was gender discrimination. She went on to attend law school but continued to face discrimination, turned down for jobs at law firms because she was a married woman. Along with Edith Green, a U.S. Representative from Oregon, and Senator Birch Bayh, Mink was instrumental in the writing and passage of the bill, as well as the later struggles over how Title IX would be interpreted.[25]

The strategy that Green, Mink, and Bayh pursued in getting Title IX passed was to say as little as possible about it and hope no one noticed the bill. The entire act is a mere 37 words that got tucked into a larger, omnibus education law. In its entirety, Title IX reads, "No person in the United States shall, on the basis of sex, be excluded from participation in, be denied the benefits of, or be subjected to discrimination under any education program or activity receiving Federal financial assistance." That's it, and that's not a lot of words for such a groundbreaking piece of legislation.

In fact, those who worked to get Title IX passed hoped that it was so short that most of the congresspeople voting for it wouldn't notice it at all. Bernice Sandler, a women's rights activist who worked with Green to get Title IX passed, told Green she was going to lobby for the bill. Green told Sandler not to meet with congresspeople to attempt to convince them to vote for Title IX for fear people would ask questions about the bill. If they asked questions, Green told Sandler, they'd find out what Title IX could *really* do. Green reasoned that if people found out what the full implications of Title IX might be, they'd never vote for it. Due in part to Green's strategy, one of the most important pieces of legislation related to gender equality slipped through Congress without much notice.[26]

Green was correct about the effects Title IX would have. Once Title IX was implemented, a whole new generation of girls and women grew up with expanded educational opportunities. This extended to all areas of education, but the bill's application to sports was especially dramatic. Before Title IX, girls made up only 7 percent of all high school athletes while today, two in five high school girls play sports.[27] Today, women make up 42 percent of all college athletes.[28] Women's sports take up 40 percent of college athletic budgets on average, a number that's still not equal, but much closer than pre–Title IX figures.[29]

In curtailing gender discrimination in education, Title IX is also partly responsible for huge gains in academic achievement for women and girls. Women now graduate at higher rates at all educational levels—high school, college, and graduate school. White women and women from middle-class and upper-class backgrounds are doing better relative to women of color and working-class women, so Title IX didn't erase racial and social class inequalities that overlap with gender.[30] That work isn't yet complete, as we'll discuss in chapter 3, but unlike Patsy Mink, women today are less likely to be denied admission to medical school based solely on their gender.

These transformations due to Title IX didn't happen all at once. It took Congress, along with the Department of Health, Education, and Welfare, several years to figure out exactly what Title IX would mean. Regulations about how the law would be applied didn't begin to circulate until 1975, and final guidelines weren't in place until 1979. But eventually, and despite Congresswoman Green's desire to fly under the radar, those with power in the sports world began to realize how Title IX would matter for them. Even though sports programs didn't directly receive money from the federal government, the colleges and universities where those programs were located did. Title IX meant that athletic programs would be covered, and this realization began to make athletic directors nervous about the fate of their male sports programs—especially football, whose large teams make achieving gender balance difficult. Some athletic programs began to make plans for how they might resist or circumvent Title IX requirements. The first such move was to work for an exemption for revenue-generating sports. With this loophole, sports programs that made money for the school—like elite college football and basketball teams—would be exempt from Title IX. Those attempts to exclude money-making college sports ultimately failed.[31]

It was also in these early discussions that the question was raised as to whether sports played in educational settings would continue to be gender-segregated. As Senator Bayh's comment suggests, one potential solution to providing equal opportunities for women and men to play sports would be to create co-ed, or gender-integrated, teams. There was precedence for gender integration at the elementary and high school levels, where physical education classes were not gender-segregated. If girls and boys could go to gym class together, why couldn't they play on the same sports teams?[32]

Those in charge of implementing Title IX also discussed whether it would make more sense to organize sports on the basis of skill level rather than gender. Rather than having a boys basketball team and girls basketball team, there would be an A league, a B league, and a C league, with the A league featuring the most skilled players, regardless of gender. This system would resemble Major League Baseball's farm system, or the way sports like wrestling and boxing match opponents on the basis of weight class.

Eventually these possibilities were discarded, and Congress decided that the best strategy would be to have gender-segregated sports at the collegiate level. Equality in opportunities for women to play sports would be achieved mostly through adding women's sports teams. The controversial aspect of Title IX was that some schools decided that taking away a few men's programs was easier than adding new programs for women. This strategy wasn't dictated by any language in the law or how it was meant to be enforced, but it still generated hostility toward Title IX at those schools which employed it.

NOT WITHOUT THE GIRLS

The deliberations about how Title IX would be implemented reveal that the gender segregation in sports we largely take for granted today was never a given. In that historical moment, congresspeople considered that perhaps the best strategy for achieving gender equality in sports would be for women and men to play together. What might the sports world look like if we'd gone in the other direction? And could we be headed that way now?

Because of Title IX, we currently live in a world where both girls and boys start playing sports at a young age. Though most programs are gender-segregated, sometimes different genders do play together. Take the example of the St. John's Chargers, a fifth-grade co-ed basketball team in New Jersey. The girls and boys on this team had played together since second grade. Ten games into their 2016–2017 season, officials with the Catholic Youth Organization league informed them that being co-ed was against the rules for middle school teams. Starting in fifth grade, teams had to be gender-segregated and so the team would have to forfeit their 10 wins up to that point in the season.[33]

The Chargers' 10 wins put them in third place in their division and they would have still been eligible for the league playoffs, but only if they played the rest of their season without the girls on their team. Parents put the question to the Chargers—should they go into the playoffs without the girls, or stick together? With a show of hands, all 11 players voted to stay together as a team. When a coach reminded the players that staying together would mean no playoffs and forfeiting the season, one of the players said, "It doesn't matter." For these 11 boys and girls, a gender-integrated team was important enough that they sacrificed larger competitive success so they could go on playing together.[34]

Title IX was implemented in a way that maintained gender segregation in sports, but the story of this team of girls and boys is still a testament to the wide-reaching success of the legislation. The culture in which the players on the Chargers team grew up is one where athletic ability and interest in sports among girls is simply taken for granted. Of course girls play sports. Of course they want to win. Of course they're exceptional athletes. The ruling of the Catholic Youth Organization league was eventually overturned, allowing the Chargers to continue playing together. You can imagine the boys and girls on that team wondering what the big deal was in the first place. That's the world Title IX created, and maybe kids like these are a sign that gender segregation in sports may be on its way out.

THE POWER OF CHEERING TOGETHER

For now, cheerleading remains one among a small handful of gender-integrated sports. But research on the effects that being on a team with women has on male cheerleaders suggests that gender integration could be a very good idea. As researchers point out, in our current gender-segregated sports system, the organization of many men's sports systems reinforces a toxic and hierarchical version of masculinity. Though not all men's sports programs are like this, many encourage a version of masculinity that is both misogynistic (hostile toward women) and homophobic (hostile toward gay men and lesbian women).[35]

This harmful version of masculinity is amplified by the fact that in team sports, men spend most of their time around men who are very much like them. This discourages the exploration of alternative ways of being masculine, and also limits men's exposure and interaction with women. Research shows that male athletes in men-only team sports are more likely to objectify women by seeing them as sexual objects to be conquered.

But sport itself is not what leads men to have this sort of attitude. One researcher followed heterosexual male college cheerleaders who had played football in high school. Before they started cheerleading, the men reported holding misogynistic views about women as athletes and women in general. But competing with women overwhelmingly changed those attitudes. After cheering alongside women, the men perceived women as good athletes who were strong, capable, and skillful. One participant said, "I used to think women were weak, but now I know that's not true . . . these women are athletes. They do stuff I'd never be able to do and I bet there are a lot of sports women can do better in."[36] This research suggests that when men and women play sports together, it can have an important impact on how male athletes think about gender.

SPORTS AND THE STALLED REVOLUTION

In the 40 or so years since the beginning of the women's movement in the United States and the passage of landmark legislation like Title IX, women have made impressive progress in revolutionizing the way we experience gender. But many men have not followed along. Researchers refer to this as the stalled revolution. More women are working than in the past. More women are achieving academic success. More women are occupying positions of power in society. Many more women are playing sports. What it means to be a woman has changed, but what it means to be a man isn't particularly different for many men.

As a group, men haven't caught up. Although the female partner in heterosexual couples may be working longer hours, the male partner has not significantly stepped up his contributions to housework and child care. With all of women's success in the workplace, men still earn more income across most jobs in the United States, and many men aren't bothered by that reality. In fact, many men direct their anger and hostility toward women and the gains they have made.

It might take a lot of hard work to un-stall the gender revolution and bring men up to speed, but perhaps the integration of sports is a good first step. The fact that sports remains a largely gender-segregated area of our social life serves to reinforce our beliefs about the fundamental differences between women and men, as well as women's "natural" inferiority. Research tells us that when women and men play sports together, it changes the way male athletes think about gender.

In the not-so-distant past, all cheerleaders were boys and being a cheerleader was a powerful and important thing. Then girls started cheering, and a lot of the power that came with being a cheerleader went away. Today, women and men sometimes cheer together and sometimes play together, and their experiences may be an important lesson for all of sports, as well as the wider world.

2

HOW TO TELL IF A WOMAN IS "REALLY" A WOMAN

Gender Testing and the Olympics

In 2009, South African runner Caster Semenya won the 800-meter race at the International Association of Athletics Federations (IAAF) World Championship, clocking the 13th fastest time in the history of the event. During live coverage of the race, a statement from the IAAF was read, stating that there were concerns that Semenya "does not meet the requirements to compete as a woman."[1] The IAAF asked Semenya to refrain from competition even though they didn't explain which requirements Semenya had failed to meet. While she waited to be cleared for competition, critics, competitors, and the media mocked Semenya as being too fast, too muscular, having a chest that was too flat, a jawline too square, a voice too deep, and hips too narrow.[2] A *Time* magazine headline asked of Semenya, "Could This Women's World Champion Be a Man?"[3] In essence, Semenya was too good an athlete to be a woman. Semenya's case, though certainly the most well-known example to date, is just the latest in a long history of gender testing for women in sports. There's no parallel interest in making sure that the men competing are really men. What explains this concern with patrolling the gender line in women's sports, but not men's?

WOMEN APPLAUD AND MEN COMPETE

For the first century of its existence as a modern sporting event, the Olympic Games had no women athletes. Pierre de Coubertin, who restarted the Games in 1896, believed that the Olympics should be focused solely on "male athleticism . . . with the applause of women as a reward."[4] But even before the modern era of Olympic competition, there's evidence of women being barred from any form of sports participation. According to Pausanias's second-century *Description of Greece*, a woman named Calipateira passed herself off as a male trainer in order to accompany her son to a gymnastic competition. When she was found out, she escaped the death sentence usually imposed for women who sneaked into the games. But in response to her intrusion, a law was passed stipulating that future trainers had to strip before they entered the arena and thus, the history of gender testing in the Olympics began.[5]

It's not surprising that women didn't compete in the modern Olympic Games until the beginning of the twentieth century. Sports have long been defined as the domain of men (and more specifically, the domain of the white, cis, straight man), a place where the ideal of masculinity can be both created and reinforced. Like many of his time, Coubertin, the father of the modern Games, believed that real women were incapable of participating in sports. The rigor and competition were too much for the fairer sex. This idea, that real woman cannot compete in sports, is one of the core assumptions that underlies the history of gender testing in sports. Women who can compete—and who excel—must not be real women, because real women are not athletes.[6]

NUDE PARADES AND DETERMINING
WHEN A LADY IS A LADY

Though there is anecdotal evidence that gender testing was part of female athletes' experience as early as 1936, the first documented case of gender testing began formally in 1966 at the European Athletics Championship. The formal testing might have been new, but the concerns about men passing themselves off as women were not. At the 1936 Berlin Olympics, American runner Helen Stephens was accused of being a man when she won the 100-meter race. Not surprisingly, these sorts of accusations often fell in line with existing global political tensions played out on the Olympic stage.[7] During the Cold War, female athletes from the Soviet Union and the Eastern Bloc countries were often accused of being men masquerading as women. Soviet women were depicted in the United States and British media as "muscular" and "hefty," while their male counterparts were "clumsy" and "working on weakness."[8] In other words, this gender reversal (manly women and womanly men) was used to demonstrate the inferiority of the Soviet Union as a place and communism as a political system.

At first, the gender testing used by the Olympics organizers and other bodies overseeing international competition wasn't much different from that of the Greeks in the second century. Female athletes lined up for "nude parades" in front of a panel of three female physicians. In the first year of its use, all 234 of the women passed, though some refused to undergo the test. The same method was used at the Pan American Games in 1967, and American shot putter, Maren Sedler, remembers vividly how traumatic the experience was. Sedler was only 16 years old at the time, and later said, "[I]t was hideous . . . and though I wasn't afraid of not passing, I just felt that it was humiliating." The Commonwealth Games in 1966 were even worse, as women were forced to undergo a gynecological exam before they could compete. The women lined up outside an examining room and were not informed ahead of time about what would be happening to them inside, where they underwent what one athlete described as basically a "grope."[9]

In 1967, the IAAF moved to a "simpler" and "more dignified" test. The IAAF is the international governing body for track and field, and in 1967 switched to a chromosome-based assessment for testing gender. The same test was used at the 1968 Olympic Games. Athletes who passed the test received "certificates of femininity," which were small, laminated licenses that they had to carry with them to all competitions and submit as proof of their female-ness. No corresponding "certificates of masculinity" were required of male athletes.

The shifting criteria for figuring out who was and wasn't a woman meant that Polish sprinter Ewa Klobukowska passed the visual test in 1966 but then had the humiliating experience of failing the chromosomal test in 1967. Klobukowska had no knowledge of her chromosomal condition and so had not set out to cheat. One member of the commission who ruled Klobukowska ineligible explained, "A lady cannot be a lady and not know it."[10] All of Klobukowska's previous medals were taken away and, at the age of 21, she could no longer compete at the international level, making her yet another victim of the gender-testing policies.

In 1985, María José Martínez-Patiño forgot to bring her "certificate of femininity" to the World University Games. That she had a certificate demonstrated that she had passed one set of gender tests. But after being subjected to an even more sophisticated test, Martínez-Patiño was informed, much to her surprise, that she was genetically a male. Martínez-Patiño's case came at a critical moment when a growing number of voices argued against the practice of gender testing in sports. Many members of the international medical community found these tests "grossly unfair" and, as early as 1969, specialists refused to administer the procedures. These medical professionals argued that the tests were both scientifically and ethically objectionable. Five Danish researchers in 1972 released a report stating that the use of gender tests in the Olympic Games should be canceled.[11]

In 1988, the International Olympic Committee (IOC) formed a working group to examine the issue. Experts like Dr. Albert de la Chapelle, a geneticist and leading expert on gender testing, took up Martínez-Patiño's cause and called for an end to gender testing. Still, it wasn't until 1992 that the IAAF declared it would stop blanket gender testing. The IAAF reserved the right to investigate female athletes in the case of "occasional anomalies."[12] The IOC continued to use gender testing and in 1992, once again changed the nature of the test. The new test defined a woman not as someone who had two X chromosomes (XX), but rather as a person who lacked a Y chromosome. Once more, these criteria revealed the difficulty in figuring out exactly what they were testing for. As the Danish researchers had said back in 1972, the IOC was essentially making its own definition of sex. Why was it so hard to settle on one definition for who is and isn't a woman?

THE TROUBLE WITH CHROMOSOMES

The problem of figuring out who is a woman and who is a man isn't unique to international sporting organizations. In American society, we mostly take it for granted that there are two types of people—female and male—and that these are real, objective, and discrete categories. This means there are criteria that anyone can use to sort people into one or the other of those categories, but not both at the same time. Prevailing norms tell us that a person can't be both a woman and a man. If gender really worked this way, determining who is and isn't a woman for the purpose of competition would not be a problem.

But the reality is much more complicated than that. Take the criteria of chromosomes, which both the IAAF and the IOC have used for gender testing. This type of test operates on the assumption that in men, the last pairing of their 23 chromosomes (what we call sex chromosomes) is XY, while in a woman, that pairing is XX. Initially, the chromosomal test focused on the presence or absence of a second X chromosome, also known as a Barr body. So those with XX chromosomes were considered female, while those with only one X were not. [13]

The problem is that not everyone lines up neatly into XX or XY. Some people are born with more than 46 chromosomes. Individuals with Kline- felter syndrome carry an additional X, so their chromosomes are XXY. Others have fewer than 46 chromosomes, like those with Turner syn- drome, who would be XO. [14] Under the initial chromosomal test, female athletes with Turner syndrome would be ineligible to compete as women, since they have no Barr body. Additionally, experts like Dr. de la Cha- pelle point out that abnormalities in the X chromosome may result in tests that are difficult to interpret. [15] In other words, sometimes it's hard to determine exactly whether something is or isn't an X chromosome. In 1992, the IOC switched away from the Barr body test to criteria that instead focused on the presence of a Y chromosome. Now, a woman would be defined not as someone with a second X chromosome but as someone *without* a Y chromosome. [16] Under these different criteria, those with Turner syndrome would now be considered women, but those with Klinefelter syndrome would no longer pass.

The shifting nature of these criteria are problematic, but as many experts repeatedly point out, they're also troubling because there is no clear link between chromosomal sex and athletic performance. If the point of gender testing is truly to prevent men from gaining a competitive advantage by passing as women, a chromosomal test of sex provides the least relevant information. For example, Martínez-Patiño failed the chromosomal test because she had androgen insensitivity syndrome (AIS). This condition affects an estimated one in five hundred athletes and one in twenty thousand in the general population. With AIS, a person's cells cannot respond to testosterone, the "male hormone." Genetically, these women seem to be male (with XY sex chromosomes as well as undescended testes), but they don't develop the strength or musculature associated with testosterone because their bodies cannot process the hormone.[17] Having AIS confers no competitive advantage whatsoever, but was still the basis for barring Martínez-Patiño from participating as a woman.

BEING INTERSEX IN SPORTS

The further we delve into the history of gender testing in sports, the more confusing it seems to get. That's because human biology is much more complicated than the simple categories of male and female imply. Chromosomal tests are problematic because our genetic makeup is more complex than the simple XX and XY that many of us presume to categorize us. Turner syndrome, Klinefelter syndrome, and AIS are some of the many conditions that fall under the umbrella term *intersex*. An intersex person is born with genitalia, chromosomes, internal anatomy, hormones, or some combination of the above that are outside the typical male/female binary. When all the different types of intersex variations are combined, it is estimated that as many as one or two in two thousand people are intersex, and these numbers may be higher among elite athletes. Some intersex variations are discovered at birth, but as the gender testing in elite sports reveals, many go undetected. Many intersex infants are altered at birth by doctors who argue that this saves these children the social and psychological distress of gender ambiguity. Intersex activists advocate for no surgery until children have reached an age to make their own decisions about their gender and their bodies. Being intersex is a naturally occurring phenomenon. Doctors often treat being intersex as a condition to be corrected, but in reality, it's simply a reflection of the natural biological diversity that exists around gender. Given that diversity, devising any biological criteria to definitively say who is and isn't a woman is impossible.

LOOKING LIKE THE "RIGHT" KIND OF WOMAN: GENDER TESTING, RACE, AND GEOGRAPHY

That it might be impossible to use any biological criteria to determine gender didn't stop the IAAF and the IOC from trying, however. In a story similar to that of Caster Semenya, Dutee Chand, one of India's fastest runners, was preparing for her first international adult track event when she got a call from the director of the Athletics Federation of India. The director was calling to ask Chand to undergo a series of medical tests to prove her gender. These tests forced Chand to demonstrate that she really was a woman rather than a man trying to gain a competitive advantage by competing as a woman. Chand had grown up never considering she was anything but female, so these demands that she prove her gender came as a complete surprise. By 2014, when Chand was informed she wouldn't be able to compete, both the IAAF and the IOC had abandoned comprehensive gender testing. But the two organizations still retained the right to test "suspicious" individuals, despite widespread protests. In practice, this policy often meant targeting female athletes who didn't fit notions of what a feminine body should look like or who were particularly successful in their sport.

These policies raise questions about exactly what a "feminine" body looks like, and how that might intersect with notions of race. Many critics have pointed out the fact that the women who have been recently targeted for gender testing tend to be women of color from the global South. Supporters of both Semenya and Chand argue that their geography and race may be the real reason for being targeted by the IAAF. Katrina Karkazis is a Stanford University bioethicist and expert on intersex issues who has pointed to the role of race in these two cases. "All of these [efforts] seem to coincide with the recent dominance by women from Sub-Saharan Africa in certain track and field events, and that wasn't the case before," Karkazis said. "That is one way this is racialized. Who is winning those events? Who has won historically?"[18] Supporters like Karkazis wonder if the IAAF would have pursued Semenya for nearly a decade if she were a white runner from the global North. These critics note that officials haven't targeted any female athletes as "suspicious" in events with a demonstrated correlation between testosterone and performance (like the pole vault and the hammer throw). That's because white women dominate in those sports, rather than women like Semenya or Chand.

Semenya's case also demonstrates the ways in which our ideas about femininity are racial and cultural. Bruce Kidd, a University of Toronto professor and longtime member of the Olympic movement, points out the way differences in men's sports are celebrated. "We encourage nations to send athletes regardless of how they look, their size and shape, and we celebrate those athletes who are at the extreme, the outliers," he said of men's sports. "In women's sport, the dominant discourse is that woman should look like the European, North American, Caucasian expectation of femininity and that they should conform to a hormonal requirement that belies the science and is not expected of the men."[19] In other words, Semenya and Chand weren't targeted because they don't look feminine, but because they don't look like a very specific version of femininity.

THE TRUTH ABOUT HORMONES

After Semenya's humiliation in 2009, IAAF officials released an ambiguous statement clearing Semenya for further competition. Speculation that Semenya had elected to take medication to lower her testosterone levels was later confirmed. In the wake of the controversy over Semenya and Chand's cases and the support they received from the public, many fellow athletes, physicians, politicians, and legal counsel, in 2011 the IAAF announced that it would abandon all language of "gender testing" and "gender verification."[20] Instead, a test for hyperandrogenism (high testosterone) would be implemented, and only when the IAAF had "reasonable grounds for believing" that a woman may have the condition.[21] Though officials argued this test had nothing to do with gender, the criteria for what constituted "high testosterone" were based on what was defined as "within the male range." In other words, women who had testosterone levels that were similar to testosterone levels in men would be barred from competition. There were two exceptions to this rule: women like Martínez-Patiño, whose bodies were unable to process testosterone; and women who took drugs in order to reduce their testosterone. Because Semenya's tests revealed levels of testosterone that were above this limit, she was told she would have to take medication to lower those levels before she could compete in the 800 meter event.

Take a step back for a second to contemplate all the implications of this new policy. First, for all its fancy language, the test is still about gender. The "normal" reference range for men is defined as between 10 and 35 nanomoles of testosterone per liter. For women, the range is .35 to 2.0. So for the purposes of testing, a female athlete must have less than 10 nanomoles per liter. Even without using the language of "gender verification," the test is based on a biological definition of what a woman is—this time hormonal instead of chromosomal.

Second, the policy forces women whose testosterone is above the limit to either be barred from competition or undergo medical intervention in order to compete. That is, women must *medically alter* their *natural* bodies in order to count as women. At the least interventionist end of the spectrum, this might involve taking drugs to suppress their naturally high testosterone levels. At the most extreme end of medical intervention, some women had their internal testes surgically removed, even though the organs posed no health risk. In at least four other cases, sports officials referred female athletes with hyperandrogenism to a French hospital where these procedures took place. The doctors also suggested the athletes have surgery to reduce the size of their clitoris, making them appear more gender "typical." In other words, the new policy led to at least some female athletes surgically altering their bodies in order to be able to compete.

But perhaps the biggest flaw in the policy is that it is based on the assumption that a certain level of testosterone in these women's bodies confers an unfair competitive advantage. If a woman has testosterone levels that are within the "male" range, she must be a better athlete than women with testosterone levels in the female range. But is that actually true?

WHAT'S THE "SEX" IN SEX HORMONES?

What is testosterone, anyway? Testosterone is a hormone, and hormones are essentially messengers in the chemical communication system in our bodies. They're released by glands or cells in one part of the body and carry instructions to the rest of the body. Testosterone is a kind of androgen and, along with estrogen, these are often referred to as sex hormones, even though both androgen and estrogen have many effects in our bodies that have nothing to do with reproduction or other biological markers of sex. Androgen, the "male hormone," is present in women's bodies, and testosterone specifically is crucial for well-being in both women and men because it contributes to heart, brain, and liver function, among other things.[22] Likewise, estrogen is in men's bodies and, even though it's a "female hormone," it can have masculinizing effects. For example, some studies have shown an association between estrogen and dominant behavior in women. Estrogen and testosterone sometimes perform identical functions.[23] As feminist biologist Anne Fausto-Sterling has pointed out, it would probably make more sense to call estrogen and androgen "growth hormones" as opposed to "sex hormones."[24]

Testosterone may not be a sex hormone, but does it still provide a competitive advantage for female athletes? As far as current research tells us, the answer is no. There is no evidence that successful athletes have higher testosterone levels than less successful athletes.[25] Studies do tell us that testosterone (in concert with many other factors) can help individuals increase their muscle size, strength, and endurance.[26] All of that seems to imply that testosterone would confer a competitive advantage, but the reality is more complicated. For example, women with complete androgen insensitivity syndrome (CAIS) are unable to process testosterone, which means the testosterone in their body has no effect on their musculature or endurance. Yet, women with CAIS are overrepresented among elite athletes, with some estimates suggesting one in five hundred female athletes are affected by CAIS.[27] That women who can't process testosterone are more likely to be elite athletes doesn't match with the argument that testosterone increases athletic ability. Additionally, women with congenital adrenal hyperplasia (CAH) have elevated levels of testosterone and therefore should have a competitive advantage. But women with CAH are more likely to have shorter stature, suffer from obesity, and face unpredictable, life-threatening crises due to loss of salt in their bodies.[28] These effects hardly seem compatible with success as an elite athlete.

The truth is that any single person is likely to have a very different reaction to the same amount of testosterone, and testosterone is just one element in a complex system of communication between hormones and our bodily processes. On top of that, competition itself, and especially winning, increases the level of testosterone in our bodies. This is true even for fans watching a game, or experimental subjects who are randomly assigned as winners. In fact, studies suggest that the relationship between testosterone and competitiveness might be the exact opposite of what we expect. In both male and female athletes, levels of testosterone in their bodies rise before a competition. The social situation of standing at the starting line has a biological effect in the form of increased testosterone. This finding is part of a growing body of research demonstrating that our hormones might be driven as much by social contexts as they are by biology.[29]

DORA OR HEINRICH?

There is no corresponding story about the gender testing of male athletes because male athletes have never been tested for gender. Unlike "real" women who are seen as suspect if they succeed at sports, "real" men are expected to excel at sports. Assumptions about female and male athletic ability tell us that there's no advantage to be gained by women trying to pass themselves off as men. All of the anxiety about sports and gender is directed at the phantom of the man passing himself off as a woman, but has that ever actually happened?

In the known history of international athletic competition, there's only one documented case of a man passing himself off as a woman, and even this story is more complicated than it first appears. At the same 1936 Berlin Olympics where Helen Stephens was accused of being a man, Dora Ratjen took fourth place in the high jump event. Ratjen was later accused of being a man and quietly returned his medal. Ratjen claimed that Nazis had forced him to pose as a woman for three years, "for the sake of honor and glory of Germany."[30] Dora's real name was Heinrich, and when his story came out, it confirmed growing anxiety about gender fraud and international sports—despite the irony that Heinrich's competitive advantage had only earned him fourth place, not a strong case for masculine superiority in sports.

For years, this story of Heinrich competing as Dora went unquestioned. Then in 2009, a German magazine reported on their investigation of Ratjen's medical and police records. Apparently, Ratjen had been born with ambiguous genitalia, or as an intersex person, and his family raised him as a girl. Ratjen dressed in girl's clothing and went to an all-girls school. He lived as a woman until two years after the 1936 Olympics. In 1938, Ratjen showed up in police records when he was arrested on a train for looking suspiciously like a man dressed in women's clothes. With relief, Ratjen informed the police that though his parents had raised him as a girl, he long suspected he was really a man. A police physician examined Ratjen and agreed with his assessment—Ratjen was a man—but also noted that his genitals were atypical. Ratjen changed his name from Dora to Heinrich, but all of those details were unknown until recently.[31] Was Ratjen, then, a man passing as a woman?

It all depends on how you define gender, and that is the critical question for sports. If you use the criteria of Ratjen's own internalized sense of who he is—his *gender identity*—then, yes, he was a man. We'll never know whether Ratjen would have passed any of the many versions of gender tests that have come and gone since then. But his case demonstrates one reason why attempts to determine once and for all who is a woman and who is a man are always bound to fail. The reality of human biology, as well as how that biology interacts with the social world, is much more complex than any simple test can explain. Any attempts to sort athletes into neat categories of female and male are bound to fail.

What's more, it is shortsighted to assume that the particular set of biological characteristics we think of as connected to gender are the most important in conferring athletic advantage. There are all kinds of ways in which some athletes are better equipped for their sports than others that have nothing to do with gender. Studies show that several elite runners and cyclists have rare conditions that give them extraordinary advantage when it comes to their muscles' ability to absorb oxygen and their resistance to fatigue.[32] Some basketball players have a condition called acromegaly, a hormonal condition that results in very large hands and feet. This condition is surely a genetic advantage in the sport, but these players are not banned.[33] More baseball players have perfect vision compared to the average population, which allows them to see the ball better than the average person when they're batting.[34] Some speculate that elite athlete Michael Phelps may enjoy competitive advantage from having Marfan syndrome, a rare genetic mutation that results in long limbs and flexible joints, two features that would provide quite the advantage in the pool.[35] In none of these sports are athletes tested for these conditions, which quite clearly confer competitive advantage. Why should hyperandrogenism be any different?

FINDING A BETTER WAY

As of this writing, Dutee Chand has been cleared to compete. The re-worked IAAF regulations released in November 2018 apply only to those female athletes who compete in distances between 400 meters and a mile. As a sprinter who competes in the 100 meter and 200 meter races, Chand is safe.[36] But under these new rules, Caster Semenya, whose event is the 800 meter race, would have to use medical intervention to lower her natural testosterone levels before she can compete. Her case went to the Court of Arbitration for Sport (CAS) and, in May 2019, the court ruled against her. This was despite the fact that Semenya revealed in her report that when she did take drugs to suppress her hormone levels between 2010 and 2015, they adversely affected her physical and mental health, and she suffered from regular fevers and constant internal abdominal pain.[37] Semenya has stated that she will not use these medications again, saying, "I will not allow the IAAF to use me and my body again. But I am concerned that other female athletes will feel compelled to let the IAAF drug them and test the effectiveness and negative health effects of differ-ent hormonal drugs. This cannot be allowed to happen."[38]

The newest regulations upheld by the CAS in 2019 are based on a French study, commissioned by the IAAF. The study of 2,127 female and male competitors at world track championship events found that women with the highest levels of testosterone performed slightly better (1.78 percent to 2.73 percent) compared to women whose testosterone was in the "normal" range.[39] But as with most of what we've discovered about the relationship between hormones and competition, the study results are more complicated than that. The biggest advantage for women with high-er levels of testosterone were in two events—the pole vault and the ham-mer throw—which the IAAF decided *not* to regulate. Additionally, men with lower levels of testosterone performed better in those two events, demonstrating again that the effects of testosterone are more complicated than always and straightforwardly providing a competitive advantage to those with more of the hormone in their bodies.

The long history of gender testing in the Olympics reveals the truth about gender as a social category in general—any biological component of gender is much, much more complex than our simple dichotomies can describe. Every biological criterion, which we believe allows us to easily sort people into two types—male and female—ends up failing in the face of the great variation of our bodies. Genitalia didn't work as a criterion, and neither did chromosomes. The IAAF's insistence on hormones as a better measure is also deeply flawed.

If all the biological criteria fail in the end, perhaps a better way might be to abandon them altogether. Some officials have suggested simply allowing athletes to compete as whatever gender they were socialized into. If an athlete was raised as a girl, she should compete as a woman. Or maybe athletes should compete based on their gender identity rather than their gender assignment. That is, athletes who feel like they are women should be able to compete as such.

As we've seen, gender testing of women in athletic competition is about much more than competitive advantage or ensuring fairness. The evidence that having higher levels of testosterone make you a better athlete is weak, if not nonexistent. Sports competition by its nature isn't fair, as athletes bring all kinds of different genetic (as well as social and economic) advantages with them onto the field. Michael Phelps was born with the long arms and legs that make him a better swimmer, just as Caster Semenya was born with her particular mix of hormones. The gender testing of athletes has less to do with athletic competition and more to do with ensuring our belief in a strict and infallible gender binary. It is a way to create and re-create the idea that there really are women and men and that they really are different. Because we test only female athletes, it also helps to reinforce the idea that women are inherently inferior at sports. Women are the ones who need to be protected from unfairness, not men. Clearly, there are no sports in which women would have a biological competitive advantage over men, right? Or are there? That's one the questions we'll explore in the next chapter.

3

THROWING LIKE A GIRL

Are Men Really Better Athletes Than Women?

Like many boys in the United States, actor John Goodman grew up playing football and baseball. He's right-handed, so when he was cast to play Babe Ruth in a film about the famous lefty baseball player, Goodman had to learn how to throw with his left hand. It wasn't easy, and Goodman practiced in private to hide his mechanics, which were embarrassing at first. Though Goodman could throw just fine with his right hand, as a lefty he "threw like a girl" until he mastered the motion with his nondominant hand. Goodman's story demonstrates what it means to say someone "throws like a girl," and it has nothing to do with underlying anatomical differences. When someone "throws like a girl, "they simply haven't learned a certain type of throwing motion. The phrase, along with others such as "run like a girl," reinforces ideas about inherent biological differences between the athletic abilities of women and men.

As discussed in previous chapters, the world of sports has long been defined as a masculine domain. For much of the history of sports, women weren't allowed to participate. Since the passage and implementation of Title IX in the United States, women have marched onto the playing field in impressive numbers. Still, it's a widely accepted assumption that in most (if not all) sports, men perform better than women. If that's true, how might we explain it? And could it be that the truth about the athletic abilities of women and men is more complicated than the simple statement that men are better athletes than women?

STRIKING OUT THE BABE, AND THROWING LIKE A GIRL

There's one event that didn't get portrayed in the movie about Babe Ruth in which John Goodman starred—the time the Babe got struck out by a woman. Seventeen-year-old pitcher Virne "Jackie" Mitchell became the second woman in history to sign a professional baseball contract in 1931. She was recruited to play for the men's AA Chattanooga Lookouts, and on April 12, 1931, the Lookouts played an exhibition game against the New York Yankees. In front of a crowd of 4000, Mitchell struck out both Babe Ruth and Lou Gehrig. Then she was pulled from the game. Just a few days later, the commissioner of baseball, Kennesaw Mountain Landis, voided Mitchell's contract. Baseball, Landis said, was "too strenuous for a woman."[1]

Maybe Landis really thought baseball was too strenuous for women, but it's likely he was also a little disturbed by the idea that a 17-year-old woman could strike out two future Hall of Famers. Virne Mitchell certainly didn't throw like a girl, or if she did, it didn't keep her from being a great pitcher. What does it mean to throw like a girl, anyway? Is there something in the chromosomal makeup of girls that dictates their throwing motion? There are no structural differences in the makeup of women and men's shoulders or arms. The case of Virne Mitchell and many other women demonstrate that not all women "throw like a girl."

As with many of the differences in men and women's athletic abilities, the likely explanation for what people mean by the expression "to throw like a girl" has to do with social factors as much as biology. In this case, throwing like a girl is due to the way girls are socialized, or how they're taught to be in their bodies. As Iris Marion Young notes,

> Not only is there a typical style of throwing like a girl, but there is a more or less typical style of running like a girl, climbing like a girl, swinging like a girl, hitting like a girl. They have in common first that the whole body is not put into fluid and directed motion, but rather . . . the motion is concentrated in one body part; and . . . tends not to reach, extend, lean, stretch, and follow through in the direction of her intention.[2]

In other words, Young is saying that girls and boys are taught to move differently. Girls are taught to be less intentional, and to take up less space with their movement.

CAN YOU RUN AND JUMP IN A DRESS?

Young's observations are backed up by research on young children in a preschool setting, which revealed observable gender differences in body movement. Girls are first restricted in their movement by what they wear—namely, dresses. It's not impossible to do things like run and throw and jump in a dress. In some sense, you could argue that dresses and skirts are *less* restrictive of body movement. The problem is that dresses come with their own set of rules about what should and shouldn't be done when wearing them. Observations of preschool-age girls as young as five years old show that the girls are already patrolling themselves and each other about how to behave in a dress. Girls pull each other's dresses down when they ride up as they crawl into and out of playground tunnels. Girls wearing overalls understand that they can put their feet up on a table, but that girls wearing dresses cannot. Dresses are often capable of being lifted up and, even at five, girls understand how embarrassing this exposure is. All of these realities of dress-wearing mean that girls spend a great deal of time and effort either managing their own clothing or having their own clothing managed and patrolled for them.[3]

Girls learn to restrict their bodies partly as a result of what they're wearing. But their movements are also patrolled by adults in ways that are much different from boys. One study found that teachers give bodily instructions to preschool boys at much higher rates than they do girls (65 percent to 26 percent). But boys obeyed the instructions of their teachers less than half the time, while girls obeyed 80 percent of the time. So even though the bodily behavior of boys was being patrolled, that patrolling wasn't as successful as it was with girls. In addition, teachers were more likely to give girls very specific instructions about how to change a bodily behavior, as opposed to more general directions for boys. Boys might be told: stop throwing, stop jumping, stop clapping, stop splashing, and so on. But girls were likely to be told: talk to her, don't yell, sit here, pick that up, be careful, be gentle, give it to me, put it down there. This difference means that boys are given a larger range of what they might do with their bodies than are girls.[4] In other words, while boys are being told in broad strokes what *not* to do, girls are being given very specific directions about what they *should* do in their bodies.

Given these findings, it's not surprising that there are big differences in the bodily movements of three-year-old girls compared to five-year-old girls. Three-year-old girls in one study were much more similar to boys of the same age in the way they played physically with other children. Girls of this age engaged in more rough-and-tumble play, more physical fighting, and more arguing. But by the time they were five, these types of rough play decreased dramatically, as girls are taught not to be "too rough" with each other. From a very early age, then, girls get less practice engaging in many of the behaviors—running, jumping, wrestling—that are crucial to many sports. A girl may be at a disadvantage long before she steps onto the field for the first time.

LEARNING NOT TO BE STRONG: MOVING AND PLAYING LESS

These early differences in how girls and boys move around matter for their sporting futures. On average, girls start playing organized sports a half year later than boys do.[5] A recent study in the United Kingdom found that boys spent 40 minutes on average on sports activities each day, compared to 25 minutes for girls.[6] In Australia, adolescent girls are 20 percent less active than their male peers.[7] In one survey of youth sports participation, 69 percent of girls reported playing organized sports compared to 75 percent of boys.[8] These differences between boys' and girls' sports participation widen with age. Many girls living in urban areas drop out of organized sports entirely. While in sixth through eighth grades, 78 percent of girls in urban areas play sports, that number drops to only 59 percent by ninth through twelfth grades.[9] Girls drop out of sports at twice the rate of boys by age 14, and this is especially true in underserved communities.[10] The opportunities for girls and women to play sports have certainly increased since the passage of Title IX in the United States in 1972, but girls still have an estimated 1.3 million fewer opportunities to play high school sports than boys do.[11] For example, in one young woman's community, the boys all-star soccer league had twice as many spots available than the girl's league.[12] That girls start playing sports later, do so at lower rates than boys, and have fewer opportunities to play high school sports are all social factors that inevitably contribute to differences in women's competitive performances.

Girls have lower rates of sports participation partly because of fewer opportunities. But other barriers are more subtle, like the social stigma that's still associated with girls in sports. Girls playing sports are still vulnerable to bullying, social isolation, or negative performance evaluations.[13] As teenagers, girls may fear being labeled a "lesbian" because of their participation in sports. Norms about what an ideal woman's body should look like make it difficult for girls to develop the muscular bodies that might be needed to play many sports. In all these ways, girls receive subtle and not-so-subtle messages that sports participation is not for them.

Society, then, makes it more difficult for girls to gain the same amount of experience as boys in sports and physical activity. These social factors interact with biology in complicated ways that make it difficult to say exactly where the social ends and the biological begins. For example, studies tell us that women have less upper-body strength compared to men, while women's lower-body strength is comparable to men's. But as discussed above, we also know that from a very young age, girls are less active than boys. They play fewer sports. Girls and women are definitely discouraged from engaging in activities that might build strength and muscular bodies. In physical education classes, teachers themselves hold stereotypical notions about girls and strength training. If women are discouraged from engaging in activities that build strength, surely these social factors have some role to play in these physical differences.

COULD A WOMAN OUTSWIM A MAN?
AVERAGE DIFFERENCES AND THE PERFORMANCE GAP

There are, of course, also some biological differences between women and men that may impact their athletic ability. But the first thing to understand about all gender differences that have been documented between men and women is that they're *average* differences, which is an important distinction to make. Let's look at height to understand what an average difference means. The average height for men in the United States is 5 feet, 9 inches tall while the average for women is 5 feet, 4 inches.[14] The very tallest man alive, at 8 feet, 2 inches, is taller than the tallest woman, at 7 feet, 8 inches.[15] But below those extremes, there's a great deal of overlap. That is, there are quite a few women who are taller than many men and quite a few men who are shorter than many women.

The same is true for any gender difference related to athletic performance. The fastest man in the world can still beat the fastest woman. But
that doesn't mean that many women cannot outrun many men. When we
talk about average differences in athletic performance, then, we have to
understand this context.

In many athletic events, there is an average performance gap, but that
gap has narrowed over time. One analysis of world records set at the
Olympics suggests that in running events specifically, women have
closed the performance gap from 30 percent in 1922 to 10.7 percent in
1984, when women's performances stabilized. That means that while in
1922, men's world records were on average 30 percent faster than wom-
en's, by 1984, men's world records were only 10 percent faster.[16] According to this analysis, the smallest gap is in the 800 meter freestyle
swimming event (5.5 percent) and largest in the long jump (18.8 percent).
These gaps mean that the very fastest women in the 800 meter freestyle
swimming event could probably beat some of the men. Focusing on
world records and the top 10 performers for select events, research suggests that the gap between women and men's performance in these Olympic events stabilized around 1983. That means that in these select, elite
events, women have come no closer to closing the performance gap since
1983. Despite predictions in the 1980s that women's times in events like
the marathon would be equal to those of men by 2000, women have not
caught up to men at the Olympic level.

Maybe the explanation for women still lagging behind men is partly
biological. But any attempt to explain the relationship between gender
and athletic performance has to include a consideration of social factors
as well. For example, all women's events in the Olympics were added
much later than men's, because women could not compete at the beginning of the modern Olympics. That means women have had less time to
catch up across all events. In addition, there are wide variations in the
level of gender equality in athletic programs on a country-by-country
basis. It wasn't until the 2012 Olympics in London that a female athlete
was a part of every country's delegation.[17] In previous years, some countries still sent all-male teams to the Olympics, meaning that there are
overall fewer women competing. An additional social barrier to women's
performance exists in sports that carry a social stigma for women. Research demonstrates that social acceptability is a barrier to women—that
is, women are less likely to participate in sports seen as inappropriate for

women—like boxing. It's no surprise, then, that women's boxing was only added as an Olympic event in 2012.[18]

SWIMMING THE ENGLISH CHANNEL, AND THE WORLD'S BEST ENDURANCE SWIMMERS

Not all the scientific evidence about gender and athletic performance comes out in favor of men. One study compared a small sample of women and men as they engaged in the same exercise, walking on a treadmill. Comparing oxygen consumption revealed that women were more efficient processors of oxygen—30 percent faster than men.[19] This would suggest that women might have a competitive advantage, as processing oxygen more efficiently lowers muscle fatigue and perceived effort, possibly boosting athletic ability. Women come closer to dissolving the gender gap in endurance events, especially those that last longer than two hours. This is due to average differences in women's bodies, which radiate heat more efficiently and more efficiently convert body fat into energy.[20]

It's not surprising, then, that a specific event in which women outperform men is long-distance swimming. Repeated analyses suggest that women have a definite athletic advantage in this field. Looking at 30 years of finishing times for the Manhattan Island Marathon Swim, a 28.5-mile loop around the city, women's times are on average 12 to 14 percent faster than men's.[21] In another long-distance swimming event, the 20.1-mile Catalina Channel Swim, the average women's times were 52.9 minutes faster than the average man's.[22] At the level of amateur open-water, long-distance swimming, the same trends hold true. The average woman is faster than the average man. Several times over the past century, women or teenage girls have held the record for the fastest English Channel swim. Women also show significant gains on men in their performance in running ultra-marathons, suggesting that in events that favor endurance over raw strength, women might be able to perform as well as, if not better than, men. In open-water endurance swimming, women's bodies, with a higher percent of body fat on average, may provide an advantage in terms of both buoyancy and protection from cold water temperatures.

Shooting is another event where performances show little to no gender gap. At the Olympic level, women and men compete separately in the rifle event. At the college level in the United States, though, NCAA events allow men and women to compete against each other. In a comparison of women and men shooters using seven years' worth of data, one study found that there were no differences in performance between women and men during either team or individual competitions. Given these findings, the policy of gender segregation in this sport at the Olympic level makes no sense.[23]

The rifle and long-distance swimming aren't the only two sports where women might be expected to perform as well as, if not better than, men. Women's higher levels of subcutaneous fat should give them an advantage in other sports where athletes are exposed to extreme temperatures, like the 1,200-mile Iditarod dog sled race across Alaska. Musher Susan Butcher has won the race four times. Women's average lower center of gravity and better flexibility could give them a competitive leg up in wrestling. In fact, as women have entered wrestling in greater numbers, they've shown themselves more than capable of competing with the boys. At the high school level, girls have won the state tournament in both Iowa and Alaska, while girls have made it to the state finals in Alabama, Indiana, and Colorado, all states where girls compete against boys.[24] Sports where having a lower body weight provides a competitive advantage—like racecar driving and horse racing—might also be places where women could equal or surpass men.

THE GENDER WAGE GAP IN SPORTS AND THE IMPORTANCE OF REWARDS

Women's participation in wrestling is a relatively new, if growing, phenomenon. In 1990, there were only 112 girls participating in high school wrestling, but by 2016–2017, that number had grown to 14,587.[25] But women have been participating in racecar driving and horse racing for much longer. If women experience a competitive advantage due to their physiology in these and other sports, why don't women dominate these events? Again, we need to look to factors beyond mere physical ability. As any athlete knows, being good at a sport is about much more than just raw physical ability. Motivation is a widely accepted part of sports performance. Everyone understands that an athlete's effort will vary based on what's at stake. The sprinter saves her best effort for the medal run, and the basketball player gives his all in the championship.

It's not a radical idea to assume that the amount of reward and recognition an athlete might receive for success at her sport could have an effect on her performance. So it's important to note that at almost all levels and across many different sports, women receive far fewer rewards and recognition than do men. Let's start with the Olympics. A successful male athlete at the Olympic level can reasonably expect to be able to make a lifelong career out of his sport, moving from competing to coaching to leadership and administrative positions in governing sports organizations. Women are still underrepresented in these positions. Take just one example: despite the success of U.S. Olympic female swimmers, it wasn't until 2012 that a woman was named head coach of the women's team. In many countries, the formal monetary award for winning an Olympic medal are the same for women and men, but the overall worth is very different. In 2012, female athletes from Australia won 57 percent of the total medals, but received only 34 percent of television coverage. Looking across all sports in Australia, only 9 percent of sports coverage is dedicated to women.[26]

In another high-profile case in the United States, the U.S. Women's soccer team signed on to a lawsuit against their governing body, the U.S. Soccer Federation, in March 2019. It was no coincidence that they did so on International Women's Day. The suit claims institutionalized gender discrimination, and asks that the much more successful women's team finally be paid equal to the men's team. The U.S. women's team has won four World Cup titles, while the men's team failed to even qualify in 2018. Despite these striking differences in results, women players are still paid significantly less. A woman who plays in and wins 20 national games would earn $99,000, while her male counterpart would get $263,320 for the same feat. This means women players are making only 38 percent of what male soccer players earn.[27] This despite the fact that in recent years, women's soccer has surpassed men's soccer in terms of the profits brought to U.S. Soccer as an organization.[28] In 2016, the year the women's team filed an Equal Employment Opportunity Commission complaint, women's soccer out-earned men's soccer by $20 million, while women players earned a quarter of the men's pay. The lawsuit also includes issues related to equal playing and travel conditions, promotion, and development.

Soccer is just the tip of the iceberg when it comes to what men and women get paid in the sports world. The WNBA's most valuable player in 2016, Sylvia Fowles, earned $109,000 for all her accomplishments. In the National Basketball Association (NBA), Leandro Barbosa was waived by the Phoenix Suns and was still expected to make $500,000, five times as much as Fowles even though Barbosa wouldn't be playing for most of the season.[29] The NBA is much more profitable as an organization than the WNBA, but even taking those profits into account, players' salaries in the WNBA make only 25 percent of the total profits of the organization compared to the NBA, where players' total salaries make up 50 percent of the profits. In golf, the U.S. Women's Open in 2015 set a record for attendance as fans watched Gee Chun win. Chun received $810,000 as an award from the U.S. Golf Association, while Jordan Spieth, the winner of the men's Open, got $1.8 million.[30] Even at the collegiate level, the university that wins the National Collegiate Athletic Association (NCAA) men's basketball tournament receives $1.56 million, while the winners of the women's tournament get nothing.[31] The only professional sport in which women are paid the same as men is tennis, where pioneers like Billie Jean King and later, Serena Williams, fought hard to be paid the same as their often less-profitable male counterparts.[32]

In sports that are available for women to play professionally, they almost always make less money than men. This doesn't include all the sports for which there are limited to no opportunities to play professionally beyond college or high school. In sports like ice hockey and football, professional leagues for women fade in and out of existence. A National Women's Hockey League currently exists, but with only five teams, there are limited chances for women to play. The Women's Football Alliance is the most recent incarnation of several professional football leagues for women, and has been around since 2009.[33]

Unequal pay is one way in which the rewards for women and men don't match up. An examination of the coverage of men and women's sports reveals even greater disparities. In one decade-long study of gender and sports coverage, researchers found that in Los Angeles, network-based affiliates devoted only 3.2 percent of airtime to women's sports on news broadcasts. That number was down from the 5 percent of airtime observed in the first year of the study—1989, suggesting that coverage of women's sports is getting worse rather than better. Looking at ESPN's coverage over the same period revealed a flat line, holding steady at 2 percent of their total sports coverage devoted to women. The blatant forms of sexism that used to characterize coverage of women's sports have faded, but chauvinism has been replaced with what researchers call "gender-bland" programming. In "gender-bland" programming, women's sports are portrayed as "lackluster" and "uninspired."[34] The exceptions to this rule are women portrayed as caring teammates, partners, or spouses. For example, one story about 2016 Olympic trapshooter medalist Cory Cogdell-Unrein focused on her status as the wife of a Chicago Bears linebacker. In other words, the tiny amount of coverage of women's sports that exists focuses on their relationships with others, rather than on their athletic achievements.

WHAT THE FUTURE HOLDS

If women were rewarded on a level even close to that of men, would their athletic performances change? What about if we changed the way girls were socialized from the very beginning in their bodies? The rate at which the performances of elite female athletes have approached that of their male counterparts slowed down in the late twentieth century, leading experts to assume that those lines would never meet. The fastest women, they concluded, would never be able to run as fast at the fastest men. Or lift as much weight, or jump as far. But is that an accurate conclusion? There's a long history of predictions about what women would "never" be able to do, including hold political office, become doctors, run a mile under five minutes, or a marathon in under three hours. Yet, women have done all of those things. The pace at which women's performances in elite athletic events have approached men's has decreased, but even slowly converging lines eventually meet.[35] Especially in light of advances in technologies that allow athletes to augment their existing talents, we can't say for sure what the future will bring.

We already know that women do outperform men in certain sports, but long-distance, open-water swimming is hardly as popular as soccer or baseball. What if it were? Is it coincidental that the most popular sports around the world are often exactly the sports that tend to reward men's physical strengths? What might a sports world look like if it were designed in ways that allowed women and men to compete more equally? How might team sports be transformed? Already, women are assumed to be better at skills like cooperation and working together, yet no one points to how those skills might give women a "natural" advantage on the football field or the basketball court.

THE KNUCKLE PRINCESS

The ban on women in the MLB created in the wake of Virne Mitchell famously striking out Babe Ruth didn't last forever. During World War II, women played in the All-American Girls Professional Baseball League as replacements for the men who were fighting overseas. Almost 50 years later, Illa Borders pitched professionally from 1997 to 2000, becoming the first female pitcher to start a professional baseball game in the United States.[36] It took another 10 years for the next woman to come along—Eri Yoshida, nicknamed the Knuckle Princess for her knuckle-ball-style pitching. Yoshida became the first woman to play professional baseball in two countries, Japan and the United States.[37] On the football field, Becca Longo became the first woman to earn a scholarship to play football at a Division II or higher school in 2017 when she signed a letter of intent to play at Adams State University.[38] Will women like these someday become not milestones to be marked, but merely the norm? Time alone won't tell. Instead, it will take proactive attempts to change structural factors—like socialization, opportunities, and relative rewards—that ensure women continue to be seen as lesser athletes.

4

SPORT FOR EVERYONE?

The Case of Transgender Athletes

In 2012, athlete and filmmaker Lauren Lubin moved to New York City and took up running. Lauren (who uses the pronouns they/them) had moved to the city to work on a documentary, *We Exist*, about the experiences of non-binary and gender-neutral people, those like Lubin who do not identify as either male or female. Lubin started running as a way to get out of the apartment in a city where they didn't know anyone, but what started as an escape soon turned into a passion. Lubin registered for their first race in 2014 and immediately the strict rules and gender segregation of sports limited them. As Lubin stood on the starting line of their first event, one of the organizers proudly proclaimed that running was an event for everyone. All the other runners cheered, but not Lubin. "I was like, 'No!' Running is *not* a sport for everyone. Running is a sport for two types of people," Lubin said.[1] Those two types of people? Women and men.

If you're a cisgender athlete, or someone for whom the gender you were assigned at birth matches the gender you identify with, you might not notice all the ways the gender binary is an integral part of sports. But if you're outside that binary, like Lubin, the deeply gendered nature of sports is impossible to ignore. In the case of running a race, everything from registration to the type of gear provided identifies runners as either female or male. Non-binary runners like Lubin are forced to put themselves into a category—male or female—that doesn't represent their sense of who they are. They must literally pretend to be someone else in order to participate. "There I was, unable to run as the person I really am," Lubin said. "Forced to either sit at the sidelines or run under a false identity in order to participate."[2]

Two years later, Lubin ran in the New York City Marathon as the first-ever gender-neutral athlete in the event's history. It's a small step, but doesn't address the mountain of barriers that face all gender non-conforming athletes, trying to find a way to fit into the gender-segregated world of sports. The deeply gendered nature of sports causes problems for many intersex athletes, as we discussed in chapter 2. Gender testing of women in international sports competition continues to result in the disqualification and humiliation of women who are naturally born with some sort of ambiguity in their biological gender. This gender testing takes place in the interests of maintaining a strict gender segregation in sports, as discussed in chapter 3. The segregation is based on a firm belief in the athletic superiority of biological males—a superiority that is supposedly based in male genetics, hormones, and/or anatomical structure. As we've explored in previous chapters, the evidence for men's unqualified athletic superiority is hardly an established fact. Still, all these dynamics converge in the experiences of transgender athletes, who are forced to figure out how to fit themselves into a sports world firmly built on the foundation of the gender binary.

RENÉE RICHARDS'S RIGHT TO PLAY

In 1976, the United States Tennis Association (USTA) announced the introduction of a gender test for women. The USTA was 10 years behind organizations like the IOC and the IAAF. The move was motivated, not by a generalized fear of men trying to pass themselves off as women, but in response to one specific person—Renée Richards.[3] Richards was born Richard Raskind instead of Renée, and with his distinctive left-handed serve, he had been captain of the Yale men's tennis team, dominated the all-Navy tennis championship, and won a New York state tennis title. In 1975, Richards underwent gender confirming surgery and became Renée. The next year, Renée won a California tournament, playing under the name Renée Clark. But her serve was recognized by a spectator, and she made the evening news because of her transgender status. A week later, the U.S. Tennis Open introduced a chromosome test, purposefully geared to prevent Richards from competing as a woman.[4]

Richards was fortunate to have the money, earned in her successful medical career, to fight back against the USTA policy. Like many transgender athletes who would come after her, Richards wanted to be able to go on enjoying tennis and saw no reason why that shouldn't be possible. Richards sued the USTA over its gender-testing policy. The arguments used by USTA lawyers echoed the nationalist fears used by the IOC and IAAF 10 years earlier to establish their own gender-testing policies. One lawyer referred to the "world-wide experiments, especially in the Iron Curtain countries, to produce athletic stars by means undreamed of a few years ago."[5] The comment had nothing to do with Richards's specific case but demonstrates the moral panic that existed around patrolling gender boundaries in sports.

Richards's case went all the way to the U.S. Supreme Court, where the justices ruled that the gender test was "grossly unfair, discriminatory and inequitable, and a violation of her civil rights."[6] Legal scholar Pamela Fatiff, in an analysis of the USTA and IOC testing policies, found that gender testing infringed on U.S. citizens' Fourth Amendment right to privacy, as well as breaching the individual's right to equal protection under the law. At the 1977 U.S. Open, Richards, competing in the women's events, lost to Virginia Wade in the first round of the singles competition, but reached the finals of the women's doubles before finally losing.[7]

THE FEAR OF TRANS WOMEN ATHLETES

Beyond the specter of Cold War, genetically modified "super athletes" from behind the Iron Curtain, the fear raised by Richards's case centered on an imagined stampede of men trying to pass themselves off as women in order to gain a competitive advantage in women's sports. Almost 30 years later, those fears persist. Most recently, Martina Navratilova, a long-standing advocate for the rights of lesbian athletes, controversially shared her belief that trans women have an inherent advantage over cis women.[8] Navratilova wrote in a 2018 op-ed,

A man can decide to be female, take hormones if required by whatever sporting organization is concerned, win everything in sight and perhaps earn a small fortune, and then reverse his decision and go back to making babies if he so desires. It's insane and it's cheating.[9]

Ironically, Navratilova had been coached by Renée Richards, after Richards beat her in a doubles match. Though she later apologized, Navratilova was subsequently removed from her position on the advisory board of Athlete Ally, an advocacy group for LGBTQ athletes. Her statement demonstrates the fear and hostility that exists toward trans women athletes.

As discussed in chapter 2, there have been no documented cases of a man doing what Navratilova proposed—temporarily passing himself off as a woman in order to compete in women's sporting events. In fact, given the gross disparities in the amount of economic rewards and recognition women receive in their sports relative to men, it's hard to imagine what would motivate a man to do so. As we discussed in chapter 3, any "fortune" women win from sporting events is indeed very, very small relative to what men can earn. Given that men are *supposed* to be able to easily beat women in all athletic competitions, it's unclear what sort of ego boost a man would get from winning in a women's event. It's difficult to brag about something you were already assumed to be able to do.

Navratilova's comments also equate being transgender with a superficial putting on and taking off gender identities in order to "cheat" at sports, an accusation that is deeply insulting to transgender individuals who face real, life-threatening struggles as they work to line up the gender they were assigned at birth with whom they truly are. Obviously, the hurtful and inaccurate nature of these comments doesn't stop organizations and individuals from continually raising the specter of men disguising themselves as women in order to gain an unfair competitive advantage. With the growing number of openly transgender individuals at all levels of sports competition—from high school to amateur races to professional teams and international events—organizations have had to develop policies to accommodate transgender athletes within this gender-segregated terrain. Those policies reflect the same concerns about male athletic advantage, with no concern about the patrolling of men's sports.

In 2003, the International Olympic Committee instituted their first policy on transgender athletes. The rules stipulated that transgender athletes could compete only after they had undergone gender-confirming surgery, followed by two years of hormone therapy.[10] This meant transgender athletes would be forced to take a two-year break from competition. It also left no room for the many transgender athletes who might not want gender-confirming surgery. As some critics pointed out, the policy could be read as pushing a form of institutionalized genital mutilation on transgender athletes.[11] It was also unclear what having or not having male or female genitalia had to do with athletic ability. In 2016, the IOC modified their policy, abandoning the surgical requirement for the participation of trans athletes. Trans men, or female-to-male (FTM) athletes, are now eligible to compete in men's events with no restrictions at all. Male-to-female (MTF) or trans women athletes, on the other hand, must provide proof that their testosterone levels have been below a certain cutoff level for at least a year prior to competition.[12]

In line with what we saw in chapter 2 regarding gender testing, the IOC's policy is much stricter when applied to women's sports than on the men's side of things. Just like intersex women, the "problem" with transgender athletes is focused around the question of how to prevent trans women from gaining a competitive advantage against cis women. This concern is echoed in the National Collegiate Athletic Association (NCAA) guidelines on transgender athletes, where the rules for trans women athletes are again different than those for trans men athletes. Trans men may compete as men regardless of whether they're taking testosterone or not. If they are taking testosterone, they need a medical exception and aren't allowed to compete on a woman's team. Trans women, on the other hand, have to go on competing as women until they've completed one calendar year of testosterone suppression treatment. For trans women who choose not to undergo testosterone suppression treatment, they are prohibited from competing on a women's team. Trans men who do not undergo hormone treatment, on the other hand, can compete on either men's or women's teams.[13]

The small but growing research being done on trans women athletes suggests that for those who undergo hormone therapy, there is no competitive advantage when they compete as women.[14] But what about trans women who don't pursue hormone suppression treatment? These policies force the broad spectrum of ways to be transgender into narrow, limiting categories. Some trans women may pursue hormone suppression treatment as part of their transition, but others may have no desire to do so. These policies leave no options for trans women who do not alter their hormone levels to compete. They force trans women into a certain way of being transgender, which may not fit their unique sense of themselves.

MACK AND ANDRAYA: THE CASE OF TWO TRANSGENDER ATHLETES

At the level of high school competition, policies on transgender athletes vary wildly in the United States. Take the case of two transgender athletes competing in two different sports in two states, with very different policies dictating how they compete. Mack Beggs is currently a redshirted wrestler at Life University in Marietta, Georgia. While in high school, Beggs was forced to wrestle against girls even though he is a transgender boy. He won the 110-pound girls state championship two years in a row in Texas, where state policy dictates that transgender athletes compete as the gender listed on their birth certificate. Even though Mack was taking low doses of testosterone and wanted to compete against other boys, state policies prevented him from doing so. It was only after graduating from high school that Mack was finally able to compete against other boys, where he won third place in the junior division of USA Wrestling's Greco-Roman and freestyle divisions.

Texas's policy prevented Mack from competing as his correct gender, and also drew objections from parents and others who felt the fact that Mack took testosterone gave him an unfair advantage. Andraya Yearwood, at the other end of the spectrum, is a runner and a trans woman who competes in Connecticut. The policy in that state allows transgender athletes to compete as their affirmed gender identity with no conditions, making it an example of one of the most open policies regarding transgender sports participation. That doesn't mean athletes like Andraya don't still face discrimination and hostility. Immediately before her race in the 2018 State Open Championship, two women confronted and harassed Andraya, calling her a boy and then shouting at her, "Why are you even on the team! Why are you here?!"[15] Andraya still took second place in the race, but then had to face parents yelling profanity at her from the stands, with some of the kids coming to her defense.

As a black transgender woman, Andraya is especially at risk of being a victim of violence. There's an ongoing epidemic of violence against transgender people, with 26 deaths in 2018. Mainstream media became aware of this trend in April 2019 with the case of Muhlaysia Booker, who was attacked by a mob and then murdered a month later in Dallas, Texas. Eighty-one percent of the murders of transgender people in 2018 were committed against trans women of color and, as of July 2019, more than 10 trans women of color had been murdered, victims of transmisogynoir, or the specific hatred of transgender women of color who sit at the intersection of three interlocking systems of oppression—sexism, cissexism, and racism.[16] All of this makes Andraya's parents especially concerned for her safety.[17] She's somewhat protected within the bubble of her small, Connecticut town, but in June 2018, a petition to change the state policy regarding transgender high school athletes was circulated. This new policy proposal, circulated by parents of female track athletes in a neighboring town, would require that transgender students compete as the gender they were assigned at birth. In order to compete as their affirmed gender, students would have to undergo hormone replacement therapy.

As the cases of Andraya and Mack demonstrate, policies on transgender athletes vary widely from state to state. Six states (Hawaii, Mississippi, Montana, South Carolina, Tennessee, and West Virginia) have no policy on the participation of transgender athletes, leaving each school district or high school free to set its own rules. With no set policy, transgender students are subject to the whim of whatever particular school officials might be in power. Nine states have policies that are outright discriminatory (Alabama, Arkansas, Idaho, Indiana, Kentucky, Louisiana, Nebraska, North Carolina, and Texas). In these states, participation is determined by the gender listed on an athlete's birth certificate, or high school athletes must have gender-confirming surgery with a hormone wait period before they can participate as their gender identity. Another 17 states (Alaska, Delaware, Georgia, Illinois, Iowa, Kansas, Maine, Michigan, Missouri, New Mexico, New York, North Dakota, Oklahoma, Ohio, Oregon, Pennsylvania, and Wisconsin) have a mix of policies that, while they aren't outright discriminatory, still present significant hurdles to participation by trans athletes. Trans athletes are dealt with on a case-by-case basis in some of these states, with subjective criteria being used to decide as which gender students can participate. In some of these states, policies mirror those of the NCAA, requiring that trans women athletes undergo a year of testosterone suppression before they can compete as women.[18]

Policies that require athletes to undergo medical intervention are problematic at the collegiate level, but they're especially dangerous for high school athletes. This has to do with high school athletics and the timing of puberty. Doctors generally recommend that transgender children not undergo any medical intervention before they hit puberty. Rather, prior to puberty, most doctors and experts recommend pursuing a gender affirming strategy with gender-expansive kids. *Gender-expansive* is an umbrella term for all children who do not conform to their culture's expectations for boys or girls. Transgender kids can be gender-expansive, but not all gender-expansive kids are transgender. In a gender-affirming strategy, family and friends support a social transition for the child. This might involve letting their child wear clothing and hairstyles appropriate to their affirmed gender, allowing their child to choose a gender-appropriate name, asking others to use the pronouns consistent with the child's affirmed gender, and using bathrooms and other facilities that match their gender identity. Because medical interventions like hormone treatment and surgery are either irreversible or can have serious, long-term side effects, most experts recommend delaying any medical therapy until after puberty, reserving these procedures for older adolescents. The logic is to allow gender-expansive kids as much time as possible to explore their gender identity before any irreversible steps are taken. High school policies mandating that transgender athletes undergo hormone treatment or surgery contradict the treatment recommendations of both the American College of Osteopathic Pediatricians and the American Academy of Pediatrics.[19]

In addition to going against expert recommendations, a policy requiring high school students to medically alter their bodies before competing as their affirmed gender makes little sense from a competitive standpoint. There are fewer gender differences in the bodies of children before puberty. At these ages, boys are not, on average, significantly taller or stronger or bigger than girls. Most of the differences in hormone levels, a concern reflected in the NCAA policy, don't emerge until after puberty. Given that these differences are already smaller in athletes before puberty, it makes no sense to institute a policy that requires them to permanently alter their bodies.

Other experts criticize these restrictive policies from a broader perspective that considers the purpose of high school sports. At the collegiate level, athletic scholarships are at stake, as well as the considerable amount of money that colleges and universities receive from their elite athletic programs. At the level of professional sports, as well, we can argue that athletes get paid to win. Perhaps if it makes sense at all to patrol against unfair competitive advantage, it would make the most sense at the collegiate and professional levels, where the stakes are higher and money is part of the game. But shouldn't a broad goal of high school sports be to learn core values like hard work, teamwork, determination, and inclusion?[20] Research tells us that playing high school sports has a wide range of benefits for student-athletes. Sports are important to developing self-esteem and a connection to both school and community. Time spent on the field or on the court also serves as a deterrent to the use of alcohol, drugs, tobacco, and other unhealthy behaviors in children and teens. Transgender children and teens are especially vulnerable to harassment and bullying from their classmates. And when they are threatened or assaulted, they're likely to receive no help from teachers, coaches, and other adults in authority.[21] More than half of all transgender youth attempt suicide before their 20th birthday.[22] These are exactly the type of students who might most benefit from participation in sports, and yet, research reveals that discrimination prevents many of these students from participating.[23] If high school sports should be about having fun and learning to work together, any competitive advantage that trans athletes, and specifically trans women, have should be secondary to the goal of inclusion.

TRANSPHOBIA AND LOCKER ROOMS

That trans girls would have a competitive advantage over cisgender girls in competition is just one of the fears that drives the policy of many high school athletic programs. This belief contributes to the stereotype, described in chapters 2 and 3, that all male bodies will perform better athletically than all female bodies. Of course, this isn't the case. As we've discussed, there's a great deal of overlap in the abilities and skills of girls and boys.

Another fear that underpins high school policy toward trans girls is the belief that transgender girls are really boys, despite their affirmed gender identity. This essentialist viewpoint might claim that trans girls are not "real" girls in the way their cisgender counterparts are. This transphobic view denies the experiences of trans girls, whose gender identity is just as real as that of cisgender people. This fear is closely related to the concern expressed by some high school authorities and parents that transgender girls pose a danger to their teammates and competitors. This "danger" takes several different forms. For some, the fear has to do with what happens on the court or the field. Transgender girls, from this perspective, pose a danger to their cisgender teammates because they're bigger, stronger, and unable to exercise adequate body control. All of these are argued to cause an increased risk of injury to other athletes.[24] This fear ignores the fact that athletes who are taller, stronger, and have less control over their bodies compete against other athletes all the time in our currently gender-segregated world. On every court and field, there are differences in size, strength, and ability. The only exception would be sports like wrestling, where weight classes control for differences of size. Allowing trans girls to compete with cis girls, then, doesn't radically alter the existing status quo in high school sports.

For some officials and parents, though, there's a different sort of fear around the participation of trans girls in sports—what happens in the locker room. These concerns echo the larger conversations in society about transgender people's right to use bathrooms that match their gender identity. The discussion clusters around two issues—safety and privacy. As far as safety goes, those opposed to trans girls using girls' locker rooms assume that transgender people themselves are a threat to cis girls.[25] These fears circle back again to the belief that trans girls and trans women aren't "real" girls or women, but men in disguise. As men, they constitute a threat to the sexual and physical safety of cis girls and cis women.

There are several weaknesses with this line of thinking. As researchers have pointed out, these arguments prioritize anatomical gender over gender identity. Because trans girls were born with male bodies, they are seen as dangerous regardless of their gender identity. These arguments presume that bathrooms and lockers room are sexual spaces, but specifically heterosexual spaces. In these spaces, anyone with male genitalia is inherently dangerous. Anyone without male genitalia is a potential victim. This narrative is both wrong and deeply insulting to women *and* men. Not all men—cisgender or transgender—are potential sexual predators in waiting. Not all women—transgender or cisgender—are passive victims destined to be the victims of violence.[26] From this perspective, allowing trans girls and trans women to use women's locker rooms and bathrooms has the added danger of making it easier for cis men who are sexual predators to prey on women in bathrooms, even though there's no empirical evidence that this is true. Of course, there's also nothing preventing cis men from preying on women in bathrooms and locker rooms under current systems of gender segregation. Simply having a sign on a door that says "women" does nothing to prevent men from going inside.

A slightly different concern about locker rooms has to do with issues of privacy. Privacy is a real concern in the open layout of many locker rooms, with communal showers and large, undifferentiated changing areas. But privacy is a concern for all students, not just transgender athletes. Many children and teenagers, regardless of their gender identity, would prefer not to be exposed in the ways common in locker room settings. A solution that would help both transgender and cisgender students would be to build different sorts of locker rooms—locker rooms designed with privacy in mind. Existing locker rooms could be retrofitted inexpensively with privacy screens. This approach supports not just transgender athletes but all students with a preference for privacy.[27]

BEING NON-BINARY IN A BINARY WORLD

Current policies regarding transgender athletes, even the most open, assume a certain way of being transgender. That is, they assume that a transgender person is someone whose gender identity is still masculine or feminine. A trans woman or a trans man can still logically compete as a woman or a man. But what about transgender people who are non-binary (people whose gender is neither male nor female)? Or genderqueer (someone who feels that their felt gender doesn't fit the socially constructed norms for their biological sex), or bigender (someone who identifies with two genders) or agender (someone who feels they lack gender, are genderless, or don't care about gender identity)?[28] People with these identities feel they are neither masculine nor feminine. Or they might feel they are some combination of both. Or they might feel like their gender is something else entirely. Where would athletes like these compete? What place is there for athletes like Lauren Lubin, with whom we started this chapter? Research suggests that the number of people who are non-binary or genderqueer is growing, especially among younger generations.[29] How will these athletes be included in a sports world that is still firmly grounded in a binary system?

No sports organization currently has a policy that includes provisions for non-binary or genderqueer athletes. Athletes like Lauren Lubin and G Ryan, a genderqueer swimmer who competes for the University of Michigan, are forced to forge their own paths through a binary system. G Ryan (who uses they/them pronouns) competes for the women's team, though team members refer to themselves as "Team 43" as a way to linguistically embrace the diverse gender identities of its members.[30] Ryan helped to install gender-inclusive restrooms and a gender-inclusive intramural recreation building on campus. They argue that sports organizations should allow non-binary and genderqueer athletes to compete for whichever team they choose. Other ways to be more gender-inclusive include using more trans- and non-binary-inclusive language; relaxing uniform requirements, which are often challenging for anyone who doesn't fit the gender norm; and building more restrooms and locker rooms that are gender-inclusive.[31]

SHOULD SPORTS BE GENDER-FREE?

Obviously, another solution is to relax or abolish the strict gender segregation of the sports world. As discussed in previous chapters, there are several arguments in favor of desegregating sports. From a historical perspective, we can compare the current gender segregation of sports to the racial segregation of sports that existed in the United States prior to the middle of the twentieth century. Before Jackie Robinson broke the color line in baseball, many of the arguments in support of racial segregation in sports echo those we hear today about gender segregation. Those opposed to integration argued that black players were inferior because they were inherently less intelligent than white athletes. These beliefs in lesser intelligence were based in racial science of the time that has since been proven wrong. In addition, scientists and other experts of the time argued that black players didn't have the necessary endurance and stamina to compete with their white counterparts. This was again rooted in scientific racism, which posited that African Americans as a race were feeble and physically inferior to the white race. Left to their own, in fact, racial scientists predicted that African Americans would die out altogether because they were so physically weak as a race.

Obviously, these predictions were wrong on many counts. As we'll explore in chapter 8, racial science today is more likely to argue for the inherent physical superiority of black athletes, though this would be just as incorrect as previous arguments about black feebleness. Few people today would argue in support of a system of sport structured along racially segregated lines, even though at the time, the system appeared completely natural. Is there truly a difference between our past system of racial segregation and today's gender segregation in sports? Are there ways in which the science being produced in support of the continued segregation of women and men might be influenced by prevailing cultural assumptions in the same way past racial science was?

As with racial segregation in sports, there are real gains to be had from desegregating sports along gender lines. Seeing Jackie Robinson and other trailblazers who came after him compete on America's playing fields had measurable effects on racial attitudes in the United States. Research suggests that degendering sports could have similar effects. When boys and men play sports with girls and women, it has the potential to change their views about what girls and women are capable of. Many all-male team sports in particular help to create and reinforce toxic forms of masculinity. Desegregating sports would provide one less location in which toxic masculinity might flourish.

There's much to be gained from a world in which women and men play together. This is especially true for transgender athletes. What's the potential cost? One of the most consistent objections is that gender-integrated sports competition would no longer be fair—men would have an unfair advantage over women. As we've discussed, this would only be true for some women and some men. There are many women who can run faster, jump higher, or throw farther than many men. But another question we have to ask is, what exactly do we mean by fairness? Are sports really fair in the first place?

If you start making a list of all the ways in which sport competition isn't particularly fair, you'll end up with a pretty long list. We can start with the all the unfair advantages that have nothing to do with biology or physical ability. Take the case of Renée Richards discussed at the beginning of the chapter. The USTA worried that Richards had an unfair advantage because she was assigned as masculine at birth. But they weren't concerned about all the advantages Richards had due to her privileged upbringing—attending a private prep school, graduating from Yale, completing medical school, and having a successful surgical practice, all of which facilitated her access to the world of highly competitive, elite tennis.[32] As a sport traditionally associated with white, upper-class people, tennis is still less accessible to non-white, poor people around the world. Social class is an important component in both access to and success in all sports because playing sports usually costs money. Sport participation is expensive because of the cost of fees, uniforms, and equipment. With today's explosion of youth travel teams in the United States, sports costs money in the time and expense it takes to get children to games, practices, and matches. At the elite level of any sport, the athletes who are still competing are there because of a cascade of unfair advantages they've been given due to their social class.

Add to social class all the other ways in which some athletes have advantages over others. Peyton Manning and Eli Manning, two highly successful National Football League quarterbacks, had an advantage in the form of a father who also played in the NFL, providing his own insight and knowledge. In fact, in many men's professional leagues, participation is passed down through family lines. Is it fair that Ken Griffey, Jr., a Hall of Fame baseball player, got to learn how to play from his father, a three-time All Star? Is it fair that NBA star Steph Curry probably benefited from the knowledge and connections his father, Dell Curry, had collected during his own extensive NBA career?

To this list of the ways in which sports isn't fair based on social factors, we can add all the other inequalities of size, speed, and ability that have nothing to do with gender. There are only a handful of sports that try to account for these physical differences in order to ensure a measure of fairness, usually based on weight class. In boxing, it's deemed unfair for a 126-pound featherweight to compete against a 200-plus-pound heavyweight. Most other sports have no size or weight restrictions on athletes. On the basketball court, is it really fair to allow Brittney Griner, at 6 feet, 8 inches, to compete against Leilani Mitchell, at 5 feet, 5 inches?

In so many ways, sports aren't really fair. If fairness isn't at stake in the gender desegregation of sports, what is? Some critics suggest that the real reason we cling to the necessity of gender segregation isn't fairness, but rather our need to reinforce the idea of gender in the first place. In a world that is increasingly gender-integrated, where the strict roles laid out for men and women are loosening, sports remains one of the last strongholds of difference. Yes, women may be able to be CEOs and hold political office and even run marathons. But they cannot beat men and they cannot play with men. Not because it would be unfair, but because it would further call into question the meaningfulness of gender as a category.

SPORT FOR EVERYONE?

Some transgender athletes have found success within the gender-segregated sports world. In 2016, Chris Mosier became the first transgender athlete to make the Team USA roster in the sprint duathlon.[33] According to IOC meeting records, two other transgender athletes competed in the 2016 Olympics, though they chose to do so anonymously. Two transgender athletes—Laurel Hubbard and Tia Thompson—have set their sights for the 2020 Olympics in Tokyo.[34] Still, when Mosier competes in North Carolina, the "bathroom bill" (HB2) prevents him from being able to use the men's restroom, a telling echo of the experiences of many African American athletes who competed during the Jim Crow ear in the American South. Activists like Lauren Lubin and Chris Mosier are hopeful that the Olympics will soon acknowledge the existence of non-binary athletes, a first step toward their inclusion and toward making sports at all levels truly open, not just to women and men, but to everyone.

5

BOW OR NO BOW?

Sexuality in Women's Sports

In April 2013, two professional basketball players came out as gay, the news about each of them breaking a mere two weeks apart. Jason Collins played for the NBA, and his first-person essay about coming out as a gay man made the front page of *Sports Illustrated* next to the bolded title, "The Gay Athlete."[1] Collins became the first openly gay male athlete to actively play in a major American men's sport. Two weeks earlier, WNBA star Brittney Griner came out in a post-draft video interview with *Sports Illustrated*. Griner was asked a question about gay athletes and answered the question by claiming her own identity as a lesbian woman.[2] The news about Griner's coming out trickled out with no headlines, no cover stories, no publicists, and no media strategy. What explains the differences between the coverage and attention paid to the sexuality of these two athletes?

Maybe it has to do with the status of women's versus men's sports in the United States. As discussed in chapter 3, men's sports receive much more media coverage than women's. That inequality would be enough to explain the attention paid to Collins versus Griner, but there's probably another dynamic at play as well. Eight years earlier, Sheryl Swoopes, another star WNBA player, came out as a lesbian with a great deal of media fanfare. She did have a publicist and a careful media strategy. Her sexuality received attention, but many fellow athletes, commentators, and fans weren't particularly surprised. WNBA player Sue Wicks, who had already come out, told the *Village Voice*, "I can't say how many [WNBA] players are gay, but it would be easier to count the straight ones."[3]

The case of Jason Collins and Brittney Griner reveals a fundamental difference between sexuality in the world of men and women's sports, as well as an important insight about the relationship between sexuality and gender in American culture. Even 40 years after the passage of Title IX and the gains in women's sports participation that came with it, sports are still seen as a masculine domain. That means that women who play and excel at sports are still liable to have their femininity called into question. Because in the United States, we believe in a strong link between gender identity and sexuality, women who are seen as less feminine are also likely to be seen as lesbians. Men, on the other hand, increase their masculinity by playing sports. In fact, as many gay male athletes have pointed out, playing certain kind of sports (rugby, but not figure skating) is a useful way to dispel any suspicions about a man's sexuality. Football players can't be gay, right? But women softball players? That's a whole different story.

THE "MUSCLE MOLL" AND HETEROSEXUALITY

From the very beginning of female participation in the sports world, questions have been raised about women's sexuality. Initially, the fear was less about sports participation making or attracting lesbian women than it was about the potentially over-sexualizing effects of sports for girls and women. These fears are part of a long history of medical science being used to keep women out of sports and other forms of physical activity. At the beginning of the twentieth century, even as many women began participating in sports, experts worried that taking the field would damage their female reproductive capacity.[4] Lingering Victorian notions from the nineteenth century about menstruation suggested that it would be especially dangerous for women to play sports during their periods, as physical (as well as social and intellectual) activity drew energy away from all-important reproductive processes. Even when these ideas relaxed somewhat, sport was still seen as dangerous to women's reproductive abilities, with the potential to cause "uterine displacement," a condition that would require surgery in order to prevent sterility.[5]

In the early twentieth century, concerns about sporting women's sexuality focused not on the "threat" of lesbianism, but rather on other ways sport would make women "mannish," a term that signified unnatural female masculinity. In addition to ongoing concerns about the effects of sports on women's reproductive capacity, experts were also worried that playing sports would unleash dangerous amounts of heterosexual passion and desire. Debates centered on whether sports was a positive way to channel women's sexual energy into wholesome activities, or whether competition unleashed "nonprocreative, erotic desires identified with male sexuality and unrespectable women." Those in charge of women's sports in that time period carefully played down competition in order to avoid inducing "powerful impulses" which would lead girls to "a temptation of excess" and the "pitfalls of overindulgence." Experts were afraid sports would make women too sexual, but specifically, too heterosexual.[6]

These debates had complicated racial and social class dimensions. In working-class settings and among some elite sports like swimming, sports promoters and organizers challenged concerns about mannishness by emphasizing the notion of the female athlete as a type of beauty queen.[7] They did this by encouraging mixed-gender audiences for events, which were often combined with postgame dances, musical contests, or outright beauty contests. Within many African American communities, women's sports emphasized competition despite fears about its effect on sexuality, even though these communities also had some sympathy for middle-class white concerns with respectability for female athletes.

Regardless of these divisions, the emphasis during this time period was on women's sports and *heterosexuality*. The dominant derogatory term for female athletes in this period was the "muscle moll," the term *moll* referring to women who were attracted to gangsters and prostitutes.[8] A muscle moll, then, was an overly strong, sexual deviant, but indisputably a *heterosexual* deviant. Though medical and scientific literature of the time often paired female homosexuality with a "boyish athleticism," physical educators and sports promoters never referred to lesbianism in their defenses of female athletes. Their emphasis on the female athletes as beauty queens in the case of sports promoters and the shield of respectability in the case of physical educators seemed to deflect any concerns about same-gender desire. This began to change in the 1930s.

The change began with concerns, not that playing sports turned women into lesbians, but that athleticism made women unattractive to men.

That these concerns gradually transformed into fears about lesbianism in sports reflects broader trends in the history of sexuality in the United States. The collapse of Victorian ideals about femininity gave way to an increased emphasis on women as overtly erotic. At the same time, the medical fixation on sexual deviance led to an increased awareness of lesbianism.[9] Whereas previous discussions of female athletes would have discussed "crushes" between women and girls who played together with no fear of the specter of homosexuality, in the 1930s, those conversations disappeared. The public increasingly began to see female athletes as potential sexual deviants—not in the sense of overly erotic *heterosexual* women, but as potential lesbians.

BABE DIDRIKSON AND THE APOLOGETIC

One of the catalysts for this change was Babe Didrikson, one of the true pioneers of twentieth-century women's sports. Born Mildred Ella Didrikson in 1911 to Norwegian immigrant parents, Didrikson's sporting career began when she was playing for the Beaumont High School team in her home state of Texas. She was spotted by representatives from the Employers Casualty Company of Dallas and asked to play for their team. At the time, teams sponsored by businesses like Employers Casualty provided one of two venues for women to participate in sports, the second being in high school and college. Employers Casualty offered Didrikson $75 a week, which she accepted as pay for being a "secretary," so that she could maintain her amateur athletic status. Didrikson was well worth every penny, as she went on to win Amateur Athletic Union (AAU) All-American Honors from 1930 to 1932 before expanding beyond basketball into track. At the 1932 AAU Championships, Didrikson single-handedly won the title for Employers Casualty, as in she was a one-woman team. Didrikson scored 30 points by herself, 8 more than the runner-up team, which scored 22 points with a team of 22 athletes. She competed in eight events, winning five outright and tying for first in another. She set world records in four events—the javelin, 80-meter hurdles, high jump, and baseball throw. In other words, Babe Didrikson was a phenom at the age of 21—and she was just getting started.[10]

It's not surprising that Didrikson's success was met with challenges to both her femininity and her sexuality. A 1932 *Vanity Fair* article called her a "strange . . . boy-child," as well as claiming that she would have been right at home in a men's locker room.[11] The article referred to Didrikson as a boy more than a dozen times and explained her athleticism as a response to her inability to attract men. The next year, *Redbook* made further allusions to Didrikson's sexuality, noting she liked men just to horse around with and not to "make love" with. The article added that her fondness for her girlfriends far surpassed her affection for any man.[12] These very public conversations about Didrikson's sexuality signaled a shift in the way people thought about female athletes in the United States. The previous concerns about sports making women overly sexual, but still heterosexual, were replaced with an association between female athleticism and lesbianism. Athletes like Didrikson became failed heterosexuals instead of muscle molls.

Not long after the articles suggesting that Didrikson was both too mannish and possibly a lesbian were published, her gender presentation changed. Didrikson had never been much for makeup, but now she began wearing lipstick, hats, dresses, girdles, perfume, and nail polish. All of these were things she had once dismissed as "too sissy."[13] Five years later, Didrikson married George Zaharias, a 235-pound professional wrestler who would become her manager. Zaharias was the very embodiment of masculinity—big, tough, ferocious, and powerful. Standing beside him, Didrikson became feminine by comparison. Thus was born what those who study gender and sports came to call the *apologetic*.

The apologetic is a way that girls and women who play sports compensate for their participation in an institution that is defined as masculine. Because they are violating gender norms, they "apologize" by emphasizing their femininity.[14] In Didrikson's case, she changed her style of dress and gender expression, making herself look more feminine. If you've ever watched a women's softball game at the high school, collegiate, or professional level, you've probably seen an example of the apologetic. You may have noticed that some players wear bows in their hair and some don't. The decision to wear a bow or not might be a simple matter of personal style, but some players and fans believe it's a signal to broadcast sexual identity. Wearing a bow is a way for female softball players to show their heterosexuality. "No-bow lesbo," is how the expression sometimes goes.

Bow or no-bow is just one example on a long list of apologetic behavior among women and girls. One strategy might be to limit their athletic participation to those sports already seen as feminine, like cheerleading, figure skating, or volleyball. Some women pair their sports participation with support for conservative gender ideology. They might suggest that a woman's place is in the home, even as they excel on the field. Other apologetic behaviors include praising the athletic superiority of men and downplaying their own athletic ability as women. In order to navigate their presence in a masculine domain, some women exclude other women who don't fit the ideals of traditional femininity, as if their lack of conformity is potentially contaminating.

Because of the ways in which gender and sexuality are seen as connected, apologetic behavior also often includes emphasizing heterosexuality. We have no access to Babe Didrikson's actual sexual identity. Perhaps her marriage to George Zaharias had nothing to do with any attempt to diffuse the veiled accusations of lesbianism.[15] But almost 90 years after Didrikson had to address accusations of mannishness, women athletes still engage in apologetic behavior. Recent research on women playing softball, basketball, and soccer at the collegiate level demonstrates that the apologetic is still a real dynamic for female athletes. When asked about negative stereotypes associated with female athletes in one study, the most common responses were that female athletes were seen as masculine, as lesbians, and as inferior to male athletes.[16] When asked about engaging in apologetic behavior, 73 percent of the women in one study reported engaging in some sort of apologetic behavior. The most common types of apologetic behavior were hanging out with men outside of sport in a public setting, trying to appear feminine, apologizing for using aggression or physical force, and talking about or trying to be seen with a boyfriend.[17] This research suggests that female athletes still feel some pressure to emphasize their heterosexuality or, in the case of lesbian and bisexual athletes, to create an illusion of heterosexuality.

THE GLASS CLOSET

The apologetic demonstrates one aspect of the homophobia that still exists in women's sports. Female athletes still feel pressure to demonstrate their femininity, which often means emphasizing their heterosexuality as well. Since Babe Didrikson's time, it has certainly become easier for female athletes to come out as lesbian. But there are still important and sometimes troubling repercussions for lesbian and bisexual athletes.

Take the case of Laura Lappin, who won a softball world championship with the U.S. team in 2010 and a silver medal at the Olympics in 2008. Lappin came out publicly before the 2008 Olympics, but it wasn't an easy journey for her, even in a sport like softball which has a reputation as being populated with many lesbian players. Perhaps in response to those stereotypes, Lappin felt there was an atmosphere that was unwelcoming of lesbian athletes from fellow players, coaches, and parents. "[Being gay] was always talked about in a pretty negative way, I would say," Lappin said of her experiences growing up in softball-dominated Southern California.[18] Lappin didn't come out until after she graduated from Stanford, and the comfort she felt in confiding to her teammates helped ease her anxiety. Still, she had to worry about how her decision to be open about her sexuality would affect her chances of making the Olympic team, or make sponsors wary of using her to endorse their gear. It's also still clear that coming out might affect the softball coaching opportunities available to her down the line. Lappin notes that the atmosphere for lesbian athletes in softball is better than it's been in the past, but still not "100 percent comfortable," which would include teammates being able to be open with each other about their sexuality, and women coaches being able to bring their female partners to games.[19]

That the atmosphere isn't 100 percent comfortable is demonstrated in several ways. Coaches still demonstrate homophobia, as in the case of Penn State women's basketball coach, Rene Portland. Portland had a reputation for being anti-gay. Her former players stated that she maintained a team policy of "No drinking, no drugs, no lesbian."[20] Portland herself admitted to as much and eventually lost her job at Penn State after being sued by a former player for her discriminatory behavior.[21] Portland is just one example of coaches incorporating homophobia into their job. Women athletes at the collegiate level still report coaches using the fear of lesbianism as a recruitment tool. Coaches using negative recruiting will warn potential athletes about lesbian players or coaches on rival teams, assuring the recruits that there are no lesbians in *their* program. Of course, in the case of many lesbian and bisexual players, this practice often backfires, as they choose a team specifically for its lesbian presence and openness.[22]

As some researchers have described, there's still very much a glass closet in softball and other women's sports. The glass closet is an informal culture of "don't ask, don't tell," where everyone knows there are lesbians on the team but their presence is covered in silence.[23] For example, one athlete chose a program because she knew the coach was a lesbian and had hoped this signaled a welcoming environment. But once she was on the team, the coach discouraged players from coming out because of her fears about negative recruiting. Another collegiate athlete reported being excluded from any activities with teammates that weren't an official team function. When she discussed this with her coach, her coach told her to try not being with her girlfriend so much. Other players may not be outright shunned, but their sexuality is also avoided as a topic of conversation in a way that isn't true of heterosexual players.[24]

CATSUITS AND THE OVERSEXUALIZATION OF BLACK FEMALE ATHLETES

Research demonstrates that African American women in sports face a unique dynamic when it comes to issues of sexuality. Black women athletes also worry about the stigma of being seen as too masculine or having their heterosexuality called into question because of their sports participation. Lynsey Jae Grace, athletics coordinator at Community College of Philadelphia and former softball player at Temple University, recalls a basketball player who was also an African American woman being discouraged from playing by her boyfriend. "The guy said, 'Why are you playing on that team? There's a lot of gay women on that team. You'll be gay if you keep playing,' he told her. And I never once saw her in the gym again," Grace said. "She quit the team because of what? I wanted to find that guy and pummel him."[25] While Brittney Griner may be an African American athlete and icon who is accepted for her sexuality, there's still an extra stigma that falls on some black female athletes for their sexuality. In addition to facing discrimination from three interlocking systems of oppression (sexism, racism, and homophobia), their families and fans may have religious beliefs that do not condone homosexuality. As Dr. Margaret Ottley, a sport psychologist at West Chester University and former athlete herself, states, "I have been in some black churches that would say, 'Hey, listen, this [homosexuality] is wrong,' and they would tell their population that."[26]

In addition to the stigma that comes with either being a lesbian or being suspected of being a lesbian, black female athletes are also more subject to oversexualization. There's a long and disturbing history of the sexualization of black women's bodies, dating back to the colonial period. Early scientists studying both race and sexuality pointed to supposed evidence in the bodies of African women to argue that they were abnormally sexual and, therefore, more like animals than their white female counterparts. Critics see similar dynamics in conversations around today's black female athletes, like tennis stars Venus and Serena Williams. The focus of much of the conversation about these two outstanding athletes is not their sports talent, but their bodies as sexual objects. Media coverage of the Williams sisters and other black female athletes focuses on what they're wearing or, more specifically, how they style their hair. One study suggests that these media accounts construct black female athletes as both sexually grotesque and pornographically erotic.[27] As a result, the potential empowerment of sports participation is always balanced against the extra burden of sexualization for many black female athletes.

RUGBY AND THE UNAPOLOGETIC

Even with these caveats, research suggests that levels of overt homophobia in women's sports has declined.[28] And while a glass closet may still exist for some lesbian and bisexual athletes, in other areas, sports participation has become an avenue to openly and emphatically challenge norms about both gender and sexuality, as well as a space to create and celebrate community. Take the example of some women's rugby teams. As a sport that necessitates certain levels of physical violence and aggression, it might not be surprising that women who play the sport often reject the idea of an apologetic. In fact, perhaps players instead emphasize an *unapologetic*, flaunting their violation of norms about gender and sexuality.

Examples of the way women rugby players can be unapologetic in their defiance of gender and sexual norms include their use of rugby songs and the dynamics of after-rugby parties. Both of these practices are adapted from men's rugby teams and then altered in ways that fit in with the gender culture of the women's teams. Rugby songs sung by men's teams are often deeply sexist and homophobic, but women rugby players alter the lyrics to reflect their more fluid attitudes toward both gender and sexuality. For example, women rugby players were likely to replace gendered terms with gender-neutral terms like "partner" and "person," which allowed the lyrics to include multiple sexualities. The most popular songs were those that were most ambiguous about sexuality and, therefore, most inclusive.[29]

Many women's rugby teams consist of a blend of women who identify as lesbian, bisexual, and heterosexual. Like men's rugby teams, women also have parties after games that include competing teams. The openness to varying sexual identities is demonstrated in one story told by a former player. Her rugby coach called the coach of the competing team to ask if they had any lesbian players. When the other coach asked why, she explained that her lesbian players wanted to go out dancing after the game and wanted to know if there were any lesbian players on the other team who might want to go along. Because of this fluid mix of women with different sexual identities, an informal norm evolved dictating that what happened at rugby parties, stayed at rugby parties. These rules create a culture that is much more open to sexual multiplicity and fluidity. In this realm of women's rugby, the apologetic—the idea that women need to compensate for being in a masculine realm—became unapologetic—a direct challenge to gender and sexual norms.[30] Women's rugby becomes a place where women don't have to hide their sexuality, but can actually explore it in an open environment.

WOMEN'S SOCCER AND SPORT AS LIBERATION

At the professional level, women's organizations like the WNBA and the LPGA negotiate a complicated relationship with the sexuality of their players. Most recently, a former WNBA player claimed the league was "98 percent lesbian" and that she had suffered bullying and discrimination as a straight player.[31] Both the WNBA and the LPGA struggle with whether to embrace the strong lesbian presence among their athletes and fans, or to ignore and downplay this reality. Meanwhile, increasing numbers of players, coaches, and other personnel have become more public about their relationships. WNBA superstar Brittney Griner briefly married fellow player Gloria Johnson before getting divorced. The female coach of the Minnesota Lynx and the female team's vice president opened up about their marriage in 2017.

Regardless of the exact percentage of queer women in these sports, and their relative openness about their sexual identity, it's true that there is a relationship between women's sports and sexuality. Why might queer women be attracted to sports given the obstacles—like the glass closet and the apologetic—we've already addressed?

Researchers have identified five possible reasons why women's sports may draw many queer women to participate. The first is precisely because of the gender-segregated nature of sports. Because there are only other women, sports becomes a space where heterosexuality is de-emphasized. Especially for younger girls, at an age when flirting with boys begins to take precedence over female friendships, sports provides a safe space for young queer women to maintain strong female friendships and avoid all the heterosexual bother over boys. The second and third reasons queer women may be drawn to sports emphasize both the physicality and the collective sharing of emotions among women. Women's sports encourages both physical and emotional intensity among women in a gender-segregated environment. This physical and emotional intensity is central to the formation of queer relationships, making it easier to find partners. Fourth, sports may be attractive to queer women precisely because they don't have to out themselves in order to participate. Lesbian and gay bars provide safe spaces for queer women, but visiting these places also makes their identities potentially public. In sports, lesbian and bisexual women can publicly enjoy the company of other women who share their sexual identity while maintaining their membership in local communities.[32]

Finally, women's sports may attract queer women precisely because it is seen as a masculine domain. As we've discussed, because of the way gender and sexuality are seen as connected, lesbianism is also seen as a violation of femininity and therefore a possible expression of masculinity. In sports, then, some queer women—those who wish to have a more masculine gender presentation—are provided with a space in which to "be themselves" by expressing their gender and sexuality in unconventional ways.[33] As we saw with women rugby players, the same is true of heterosexual women. Because lesbian women are excluded from notions of "real" womanhood, sports provides them with an opportunity to invent their own definition of what womanhood might look like. For all these reasons, sports can become an affirming place for lesbian and bisexual women. One study of lesbian youth involved in sports found that their participation allowed them to affirm that there were other people like them, as well as that their attraction to other women was okay. [34]

If the example of the 2019 U.S. Women's National Team (USWNT) for the World Cup is any indication, the climate around sexuality and women's sports is definitely changing. The USWNT alone had five openly queer players: Megan Rapinoe, Adrianna French, Tierna Davidson, Ali Krieger, and Ashlyn Harris. Krieger and Harris are engaged to each other, while Rapinoe's girlfriend, Sue Bird, plays for the WNBA. There were 34 queer women competing across all teams in the most recent FIFA Women's World Cup, along with one coach (Jill Ellis, coach of the USWNT) and one trainer. Queer players like Megan Rapinoe achieved sports superstar status leading up to and in the aftermath of the women's successful defense of their fourth World Cup title. Rapinoe became the first out lesbian to pose for the *Sports Illustrated* swimsuit issue. The same month, players from the USWNT were featured in a Nike ad campaign, with sprawling billboards in prominent locations in downtown New York and Los Angeles.

Given their fearlessness on issues of both sexuality and gender equality, it's no surprise that queer fans have embraced the team. Writer and humorist Jill Gutowitz remembers her first experience with USWNT fandom. In 2015, a friend invited her to a bar to watch the women's team play. As she describes it, "The bar was packed with queer women, painted red, white and blue, even donning U.S. Women's National Team jerseys with the names of players on their backs: Rapinoe, Lloyd, Morgan. I had never seen anything like it; it was like an all-lesbian reboot of your local sports bar on any given Sunday." [35] Gutowitz spoke with other queer women about the appeal of the USWNT. For some, it's about their physical attractiveness—specifically, the muscular soccer woman legs. Others describe wanting to be like team members in terms of their style and confidence. Some queer fans are sporty, but the appeal of the USWNT transcends the sporty versus non-sporty divide. Molly Priddy, a 33-year-old writer, described to Gutowitz what the USWNT means to her: "When I was growing up, the idea of dykes in sports scared all the parents—who would be in the changing rooms with the other girls?

Wouldn't they be predatory in that environment? The answer, obviously, is no, but being an openly gay athlete was and is still a gamble for many athletes. So for these soccer players to be at the top of their game, quite literally, and be open about their sexuality? It's powerful."[36]

FROM BABE TO MEGAN

Our ideas about women, sports, and sexual identity have changed a great deal in the years between Babe Didrikson and Megan Rapinoe. What does the future hold for sexuality in women's sports? Will the glass closet disappear altogether? Will the need for any apologetic fade over time? As we've seen, these questions are inexplicably linked to the gendered nature of sports. As a masculine domain, the perception that women must give up some of their femininity in order to play persists. As we'll see in the next chapter, the experience for gay men in sports has a very different trajectory.

6

INSIDE THE BOYS' LOCKER ROOM

Homophobia and Men's Sports

In 2015, Michael Sam became the first openly gay NFL player in the history of the league. Sam entered the NFL with an outstanding college career, earning his conference's Defensive Player of the Year award, first team All-American, and being voted by his teammates as the University of Missouri's most valuable player. He'd already come out to his teammates and coach, who were all deeply supportive. Shortly before the NFL draft, Sam came out to the rest of the world and despite his college performance, was drafted in the seventh round by the St. Louis Rams. His professional career was short-lived, as he was cut from teams, first in St. Louis and then in Dallas. After a brief stint in the Canadian Football League, Sam quit the sport, citing in part the difficulty that came with being a gay man in football.

Though some in the LGBTQ+ community hoped Sam would become the Jackie Robinson of the sports world for gay men, that's not how the story ended. Critics speculated whether Sam's sexual identity affected his career. Sam performed well in pre-season games with St. Louis before being let go. Did his status as a gay man factor into that decision? In the four years since Sam's brief time in the NFL, no players have followed in his footsteps.[1] Sam's story illustrates several of the important dynamics that come into play when considering men's sports and sexuality. Acceptance of homosexuality among male athletes is increasing, especially at the high school and collegiate level, as the reaction of Sam's college teammates demonstrates. But though progress has been made in some areas, there's still a long way to go toward ending the homophobia that is deeply embedded in the locker room and on the field in men's sports.

SPORT AND THE MAKING OF MEN

In previous chapters, we've discussed how sports is seen as a masculine domain. We haven't yet explored exactly how that came about. Perhaps asking how and why sports are so deeply associated with masculinity doesn't even seem like a question that needs to be asked. It's just the way it is. But as with many of the truths we take for granted about gender, the close connection between masculinity, sports, and sexuality has a very specific history. In order to understand that complicated relationship, we have to first unpack how sports became associated with masculinity.

The story of masculinity and sport begins with the Industrial Revolution, a period that historians argue is when sports becomes culturally important in places like the United States and Great Britain. Up until that point, sport wasn't seen as a means of character improvement or crucial to the moral and physical health of society. Sport, as a leisure activity, was mostly reserved for the small slice of the population who had the luxury of time to spend doing something besides working—the aristocracy. With the Industrial Revolution, that changed. Sport spread across social classes, and became an important means of instilling the values needed to create a docile and compliant workforce. Youth sports then, as now, were sponsored by businesses who had a vested interest in young people learning how to keep a schedule under the supervision of production-conscious supervisors—a skill these businesses believed sports could teach.[2]

Sports helped to create good workers, but specifically good *male* workers. The Industrial Revolution had important gender consequences. The doctrine of separate spheres that developed during this period dictated that men would do paid work outside the home while women's domain would be within, performing the unpaid labor of taking care of the home and children. With more and more men working in factories or offices instead of farming or testing their mettle on the American frontier, many social commentators feared that men were going soft. Because the home was now a feminine space and fathers were working outside of the home, boys lacked the intense contact with adult men needed to make them sufficiently manly. This cultural hysteria was directly related to fears, not just that men wouldn't be manly enough, but that they would become homosexual.[3]

Enter Theodore Roosevelt, who told an audience in 1903, "I believe in rough games and in rough, manly sports. I do not feel any particular sympathy for the person who gets battered about a good deal so long as it is not fatal."[4] Football during this time period certainly fit the bill as a rough sport. The problem was that it was a bit too fatal. In 1904 alone, there were 18 reported football deaths, and 159 serious injuries. Players had little protective equipment and so suffered gruesome injuries, including wrenched spinal cords, crushed skulls, and broken ribs that pierced their hearts. After what the *Chicago Tribune* called a "death harvest" season in 1905 (with 19 player deaths and 137 serious injuries), Stanford and California switched to rugby over football, while Columbia, Northwestern, and Duke dropped their football teams altogether. Roosevelt used his pulpit to call for rule changes that would reduce the number of fatalities and injuries in the sport, and these changes happened in 1906.

Football was worth preserving because it would help American men develop the "courage, resolution, and endurance" necessary to win not just on the field, but on the global stage. According to Roosevelt, all the "masterful nations" of the world encouraged rugged sports. Football, then, was important not only to the preservation of proper masculinity, but to the nation as a whole. Though another spike in fatalities in 1909 necessitated more rule changes, football was saved and cemented as a place where players could learn to be real rough-and-tumble men, safe from the feminizing influence of women and the dangers of homosexuality.[5]

ORTHODOX MASCULINITY AND HOMOPHOBIA

Roosevelt and others working to save football were contributing to the development of a particular form of masculinity, what some scholars call *orthodox masculinity*. Orthodox masculinity goes hand in hand with many sports. The characteristics of orthodox masculinity include risk-taking, self-sacrifice, marginalizing of others, a willingness to inflict bodily damage, the acceptance of pain and injury, and a disparaging view of femininity. Most important for our discussion is homophobia, the final component of orthodox masculinity. Orthodox masculinity is reproduced within many men's sports because of the ways in which sports serve as a near-total institution. That is, sport is a nearly enclosed social system that controls many aspects of an athlete's life. Men's participation in sports in many ways resembles the military, playing up myths of glory, patriotism, and masculinity within a rigid hierarchical structure that limits individual freedom in order to enforce ideas of orthodox masculinity. Because sports, especially at the collegiate and professional levels, take up so much of an athlete's time, players are mostly prevented from encountering any alternative forms of masculinity. These athletes also spend much larger chunks of their time only with other men who are also invested in orthodox masculinity. Their limited exposure to both other forms of masculinity and women narrows their range of possible identities, strengthening the hold of orthodox masculinity.[6]

FROM AESTHETICS TO ATHLETICISM: MASCULINITY IN FIGURE SKATING

Sports like football are strongholds for orthodox masculinity, and by the early twentieth century, American football had cemented its position as the preserver of masculinity, heterosexuality, and nationalism. It's no surprise, then, that Michael Sam is still the only openly gay player in the history of the NFL. But do all sports support orthodox masculinity to the same degree? In the United States, football is firmly entrenched at the top of the hierarchy of orthodox masculinity, followed by sports like baseball, basketball, hockey, and boxing. Around the rest of the world, soccer is more likely to be seen as the premier masculine sport. At the bottom of those lists, with a great deal of variation depending on where you live and your own experiences, might be sports like golf, tennis, gymnastics, cheerleading and, of course, figure skating. Figure skating, with its costumes, music, artistry, and close association to dance make it more like ballet than a sport, and therefore less masculine. Like football, the femininity of figure skating appears to be a taken-for-granted truth. Figure skating is less masculine, and it's always been that way. But as with football, there's a specific history to how figure skating came to be seen as both less masculine and therefore more likely to include gay athletes, though as we'll see, it is still perhaps no more friendly to openly gay athletes.

Figure skating began very much as an activity for men, specifically for upper-class men. Early skating clubs included members of the aristocracy and were seen as a way to express the grace and beauty that were important characteristics of masculinity for that social class. Unlike other sports, figure skating didn't develop out of the Victorian "cult of athleticism." Similar to Roosevelt's ideas about football in the United States, this cult of athleticism saw sports as a way for boys to develop important masculine traits like physical vigor, courage, and tenacity.[7] The cult of athleticism very much still persists in our contemporary ideas about sports and masculinity. But figure skating developed instead from a refined view of masculinity that was meant to produce a "man of feeling." This man privileged qualities such as politeness, sensibility, and expressiveness.[8] Emerging from this tradition allowed early male figure skaters to emphasize the beauty of their sport as much as its physicality or the courage required.

In the 1800s, women entered figure skating in large numbers, though the activity continued to be the preserve of mainly upper-class individuals. It was during this period that one of the primary tensions in figure skating developed—that between figure skating as an art and as a sport. As an art, figure skating was a way to demonstrate important boundaries between the aesthetic sensibilities of the upper class compared to the middle class and working class. It was partly figure skating's ambiguous status that made it acceptable for women to participate. Sport during this time period was strictly off-limits for women. Women were allowed on the ice, but they still weren't in charge. Men drove the gradual shift from art to sport in the nineteenth century. The balance tilted toward competitive sport over art as figure skating became more influenced by middle-class sensibilities. However, it was still a very different kind of sport, in that competition was judged largely on artistry and aesthetic ability. In these early days, figure skating was one of the few sports where women competed directly against men.

In fact, figure skating was unique in that for a short period of time in the early twentieth century, it became a mostly gender-neutral sport. The special qualities of figure skating made it a place where women could hold their own against men. It was a sport, yes, but not one characterized by the homosocial, male bonding of team sports. Figure skating certainly requires strength and agility, but is also judged on aesthetics. The costumes worn by women in figure skating allowed them to still be seen as feminine in a sporting context. All of these factors meant that for a brief moment, figure skating was seen as neither masculine nor feminine. That changed in the 1930s with the influence of one athlete—Sonja Henie. The Norwegian skater dominated the sport in the 1920s and 1930s, along with a cohort of female skaters responsible for important stylistic and technical advances. By the end of World War II, figure skating was no longer gender-neutral, but dominated by women and concerned about its "boy problem," or the lack of men and boys in the sport. Like cheerleading, discussed in chapter 1, figure skating transitioned from a men's sport to a gender-neutral sport and then a women's sport in a relatively short period of time.

That complicated relationship between masculinity and figure skating persists into the twenty-first century. In 2018, figure skaters Adam Rippon and Eric Radford together became the first openly gay male athletes to ever win medals at the Winter Olympics.[9] Rippon and Radford weren't by any means the first gay figure skaters. In 1976, British figure skater John Curry won gold at the Olympics and afterward was interviewed by the Associated Press. Curry revealed his sexual identity to the reporter under the assumption that it was off the record, but the information was included in the story, outing Curry to the world. In the media, his sexuality quickly overwhelmed any other aspects of Curry's identity, including his radical and revolutionary skating, his alluring artistry, or the history of abuse he'd faced in the sport due to his sexuality. Curry revealed the ways in which coaches had tried to curb what they deemed as more "flamboyant" gestures in his skating:

> When I started to skate, I had a coach who used to grab my arm and push it back to my side when I finished a movement with it in the air. . . . This man wanted me to skate in a certain way and when I didn't, he beat me. Literally beat me. And there were more humiliating things. He sent me to a doctor as if there were something to treat.[10]

One coach told Curry, after they parted ways, that Curry would never make it as a skater or a man. After the interview, Curry became a haunted hero and a lesson to other closeted gay male skaters on the circuit.[11] There were consequences for coming out or for pushing the boundaries of the sport, and they weren't good.

Twenty years later, Rudy Galindo, a Mexican American pairs figure skater, still felt the same pressures when he came out. He describes being put under a microscope and the ways in which the power brokers within the sport tried to contain him.[12] As described by one reporter, figure skating had become gendered in a more subtle way by making distinctions between more "athletic" (i.e., masculine) and "artistic" (i.e., effeminate) men. Being athletic, and therefore masculine, was rewarded, while being artistic and therefore effeminate was punished. In the same time period, critics of the sport attributed its declining popularity in part to its "gay reputation," while others suggested that judges punished gay male figure skaters with a subtle homophobic bias.[13] Galindo and others hope that with openly gay skaters like Rippon and Radford, the sport has finally turned a corner so that gay male skaters can be out without suffering any of the negative consequences faced by previous generations.

Figure skating isn't the only sport that has experienced progress in its acceptance of gay male athletes. Research on the experiences of openly gay male athletes in high school and college in the United States demonstrates significant progress since the beginning of the twenty-first century. In a comparison of interviews with gay athletes in 2002 to a cohort in 2010, openly gay men playing high school and college sports experienced considerably less heterosexism.[14] In 2002, most of the athletes who were out feared violence, bullying, discrimination, and/or harassment from their teammates. In 2010, athletes like Charlie, a soccer player in California, could say, "I've never bothered to be anything other than out. And nobody, I mean nobody, has cared."[15] In 2002, all the gay male athletes in the study heard the word "fag," as well as phrases like "that's so gay," frequently. By 2010, athletes heard these less often and some reported that homophobic words and phrases were not used at all. The level of acceptance on some teams was demonstrated by the fact that gay athletes could talk openly about their sexuality with their teammates. The environment in which gay athletes are still less likely to come out is in cases of dealing with a homophobic coach.

COLLISION VERSUS DECISION: BLACK GAY MALE ATHLETES

Rudy Galindo, in addition to facing discrimination as a gay athlete, also had to deal with being Mexican American in the predominantly white sport of figure skating. Sexuality, gender, and race intersect in interesting ways to influence who is likely to compete in different sports. Black men are associated with highly competitive and combative sports like basketball and football, or with individual sports that require strength and explosiveness, like sprinting and boxing. Gay male athletes, as we've discussed, are linked to sports that are perceived as more feminine, like figure skating, cheerleading, and gymnastics. Sports associated with African American men are about collision, whereas "gay" male sports are determined by decision.[16] These separate categories suggest that there's no overlap between black male athletes and gay male athletes—that these are incompatible categories.

Some research does point to the increased homophobia that queer black men sometimes face from within the African American community. Most studies find increased amounts of homophobia among black people.[17] This dynamic is explained in part by denial of queer women and men within some African American communities. Denying the existence of queer black men and women allows some black people to view homosexuality as "white people's problem." In the sports world specifically, one survey found elevated levels of homophobia among black athletes compared to white athletes at three major Southern universities.[18] In an interview of 175 rookie NFL players commissioned by professional sports agent Ralph Cindrich, 92 percent of white players said they would feel comfortable with a gay teammate. This compares to 60 percent of black players who said they'd be okay with a gay teammate. Among white players, 53 percent would be fine sharing a hotel room with a gay teammate, compared to 29 percent of black players. Finally, when athletes were asked how they would react to being propositioned by a gay player, 5 percent of white players said they would respond with a physical assault, compared to 29 percent of black players.[19] These realities potentially make the experiences of black male gay athletes even more difficult.

Of course, as we've seen, there are black, gay male athletes in team sports. Jason Collins, who came out at the end of his NBA career, and

Michael Sam are both African American. If gay men in general are under-represented in sports, gay black men are even more so. Years after leaving the NFL, Sam talked about the racism he's experienced from the gay community, being told he's not black enough or gay enough.[20] For Sam, these sentiments have come mainly from the gay community, while he's had a much more accepting experience from within the black community. When Derrick Gordon, an African American basketball player at the University of Massachusetts, came out as gay in 2014, he received a great deal of support from fellow students. When five members of Westboro Baptist church showed up to condemn Gordon, 1,500 students demonstrated in support of him.[21] One study of students at the University of Toronto found no difference between levels of prejudice toward gay people among black and white students, suggesting that any racial disparities in views toward homosexuality probably vary based on context and setting.[22]

THE MISSING MEN

Perhaps these gains at the level of high school and college sports will soon trickle up into men's professional leagues as well. So far, this hasn't been the case. In addition to Michael Sam, 11 other NFL players have been identified as gay, all except Sam coming out only after their career was over. No NFL player has come out while he was actively on a team.[23] In the NBA, Jason Collins remains the only professional athlete in the big four leagues (MLB, NBA, NFL, NHL) to come out while actively playing, joining John Amaechi as the only other out NBA player. Glenn Burke and Billie Bean are the only two Major League Baseball players to come out, both after retirement. No players in the National Hockey League have come out to date.[24] With Robbie Rodgers's retirement and Collin Martin's transfer out of Major League Soccer, there are now no active gay players in MLS and, in fact, no active, out gay players in any of the major professional men's sports leagues in the United States. This means that among the roughly 3,000 men currently playing professional sports in the United States across all five leagues, not one is openly gay.

At the global level, Justin Fashanu, a British soccer player, came out in 1990, before his eventual retirement in 1997. Fashanu was shunned by the global soccer world, including his brother, and committed suicide in

1998.[25] In 2014, Thomas Hitzlsperger came out after his retirement, becoming the first English Premier League soccer player to do so.[26] The only out, male soccer player currently is Sweden's Anton Hysen. As recently as 2018, France's World Cup–winning striker Olivier Giroud said he believed it would be "impossible" for a male soccer player to come out.[27]

Doing the math on these numbers just within the United States means that only about .03 percent of professional contracts have been signed by men ever known to be gay. The patterns are similar for European soccer leagues, as well as individual sports like tennis and boxing. This figure, .03 percent, is much smaller than the estimates of gay men in the general population, which is about 2.8 percent on average.[28] If the percentage of gay men playing professional sports came even close to mirroring the general population, there should be a lot more gay athletes. Where are those missing men? There are two possible explanations for why gay men aren't represented in professional sports in the same ratio as they are in the general population.

The first explanation is the homophobia hypothesis. From this perspective, the percentage of gay men playing professional sports is closer to the percentage in the population than the numbers suggest. The missing men are those athletes who choose to remain silent because of the homophobic nature of the leagues and organizations in which they compete. The fact that many players choose to wait until after they retire to come out lends support to the homophobia hypothesis. The homophobia encountered by gay male athletes can take different forms. They may encounter direct, overt hostility based on intolerant attitudes toward homosexuality. Or perhaps most of their team is supportive, but one player or coach is enough to persuade an athlete not to come out. Gay male athletes may choose not to come out, not because of homophobic attitudes, but because they fear they'll be perceived as different in a way that affects team cohesion. That is, if they come out, they'll no longer be included in the locker room camaraderie. Moreover, in the deeply competitive environment that is elite sports, athletes who stand out in any way risk being punished by losing their starting position, endorsements, or being released from their team.[29]

There may also be a generational aspect to the homophobia encountered by gay male athletes. Younger generations are increasingly open to homosexuality, but the older men in decision-making positions in elite sports are still those who came of age in a time with much higher levels of homophobia. Coaches, managers, executives, and owners have the power to dictate the careers of athletes, and so it may be strategically wise to keep one's sexual identity hidden.

Further evidence in support of the homophobia hypothesis suggests that gay athletes are selective about to whom they come out. They might be open to their teammates, but not to the media. Some evidence for this exists in the fact that researchers who study sport and sexuality have knowledge of players who are out to their team, but not to the rest of the world. For example, the NCAA American football player, Alan Gendreau, was out to his team and to sport researcher Eric Anderson several years before coming out to the media.[30] Michael Sam, too, was out to his team before coming out in a more public manner. A 2014 article claimed that globally, at least eight professional male soccer players were out to their teammates but not the media, and seven of the players claimed that they had chosen to stay quiet because of the backlash that was likely to come from fans.[31]

This state of being selectively out might explain why rumors seem to swirl around certain professional players regarding their sexuality. In the NFL, superstars Troy Aikman, Odell Beckham, Jr., Aaron Rodgers, and Tim Tebow have fielded questions at various points about their sexuality.[32] Two out of the eleven gay NFL players on record—Jerry Smith and Ray McDonald—never openly discussed their homosexuality, even after they left the league.[33] McDonald was arrested for having sex with a man in 1968, which was still a criminal act at the time. Dave Kopay, a gay NFL player who came out after his retirement, was aware of both McDonald and Smith's homosexuality but revealed his knowledge only after their deaths.[34] The case of these athletes may suggest that being selectively out happens more often than the numbers suggest.

The second explanation for gay athletes' under-representation is the nonparticipation hypothesis. Simply put, there are, in fact, fewer gay men in professional sports because most gay men are not drawn to those professions. Gay men are overrepresented in other activities—such as theater, music, dancing, and art—and there are only so many gay men with so much time. Gay men engaged in these other activities reduce the number of gay men available to play sports. Of course, there are concrete reasons why gay men might gravitate toward theater or dancing over football or baseball—because the world of dancing and music are more welcoming to gay men. The missing men in professional sports is probably best understood as resulting from both of these factors—homophobia and nonparticipation. As a new generation of young people who are more open about sexuality come to power in professional men's sports, will the representation of gay men increase?

GAY CLUBS AND RECREATIONAL SPORTS

While openly gay men in elite professional sports are few and far between, the culture of gay men's recreational sports clubs is diverse and rich. In the United Kingdom, the Gay Football Supporters Network (GFSN) was founded as a nonprofit in 1989 by a small group of gay soccer fans in response to the homophobia experienced by gay players and fans in the sport. The organization has three pillars: supporting, playing, and campaigning. Supporting aims to provide support for LGBT soccer fans by gathering together to talk about, watch, or attend soccer events. The GFSN campaigning component works for more acceptance of LGBT players and fans within the soccer world in general.[35] The playing arm of the organization created the only national gay soccer league, with 22 teams in two different divisions.[36] Teams compete both against other clubs within the GFSN network and other traditional soccer clubs.

Gay sports clubs meet several different needs for their participants. They provide a space for gay athletes to compete free from the homophobia that characterizes other clubs. They also help create community, fostering friendships as well as a place to meet potential sexual and romantic partners. Not surprisingly, these different orientations sometimes come into conflict. On some teams, tensions emerge between players who are focused on the competitive aspect of participation—beating other gay and "straight" teams—and those who are there mostly for romance, friendship, and community. The emphasis on winning for some players and teams has led to an interesting dynamic in which gay clubs become "infiltrated" by straight players. These straight players exhibit inclusive attitudes toward homosexuality, but their numbers have become widespread enough that in the United States, some clubs have passed rules limiting the number of straight players allowed on a team.[37]

One study of gay men's clubs and leagues suggests that when it comes to challenging homophobia and orthodox masculinity, gay soccer players find themselves in something of a bind. Players are most successful in challenging stereotypes about gay men in sports when they adopt exactly those masculine traits and behaviors that have been previously used to exclude them. For example, one player on a Dublin soccer club noted that the team had developed a reputation within the local league for being a "bit rough" in their play.[38] He speculated that this might be due to gay players overcompensating, saying that

> it's not that we're rough in a disrespectful way, maybe it's an element of the team that almost overcompensated for being gay, tried to throw in an extra element of masculinity on the pitch in a kind of slightly more aggressive, challenging fashion.[39]

On another team, the coach patrolled his teammates for any behaviors that violated orthodox masculinity, telling them not to refer to each other as "girls" on the sidelines if they wanted to be respected as a real football team. In other words, if gay men want to be respected on the soccer pitch, they had to be sure to suppress any behaviors that didn't conform to orthodox masculinity. The researcher concludes that though the exclusively gay clubs and leagues serve an important function for the LGBT community, those teams who play against straight teams do more to challenge stereotypes about sport and sexuality, even if they leave certain elements of masculinity unchanged.

BROMANCES, CUDDLING, AND STRAIGHT ATHLETES

There is some evidence that the form of orthodox masculinity is changing within men's sports in certain places. Research on straight men in sports suggests that as homophobia decreases, straight men feel more comfortable expressing emotional intimacy without fear of being homosexualized. Studies in the United Kingdom suggest that it's becoming more acceptable for male teammates to express "very high levels of affection for each other," with no need to qualify their statements as heterosexual.[40] This applies to physical affection as well. In the British soccer world, the sight of two straight men kissing each other to celebrate a goal or a victory has become much more common, without any repercussions to the players' sexuality.[41] Research suggests in this context, straight men kissing other straight men has been stripped of its sexual significance, becoming no different than a handshake. In the United Kingdom, cuddling, spooning, and sharing beds with other men are all also becoming more acceptable without the stigma of homosexuality. In the United States, straight young men haven't quite caught up to the increasingly relaxed norms of their British counterparts. This might be due to a cultural lag, in which young men express support for homosexuality in general, but aren't ready to start cuddling with their teammates.[42] With time, perhaps the homophobic component of orthodox masculinity will fade for American men as well, leaving them more room to escape the strict confines of that role.

The reality is that, for the moment, masculinity is still closely tied to heterosexuality. In order for gay men to be more accepted in sports, either that definition of masculinity has to change, or sport needs to become less masculine as an institution. On the surface, gay men's participation shouldn't challenge the gender norms of sports. Being gay is about who a person is attracted to, and not about their gender. But because of the way gender and sexuality are interwoven, gay men's inclusion in sports is still perceived as a threat to masculinity.

7

WHY THE DUTCH ARE
SO GOOD AT BASEBALL

Globalization, Sports, and the Legacy of Colonialism

If someone asked you to name the countries with the best national baseball teams, would the Netherlands be at the top of your list? There are many things the small European nation of the Netherlands is known for—tulips, windmills, and wooden shoes. But baseball probably isn't one of them. Nevertheless, in 2011 the Kingdom of the Netherlands' national baseball team beat the Cuban national team to win the World Baseball Classic, an international competition modeled on soccer's World Cup. How did the Dutch get to be so good at baseball?

The answer lies on a tiny island in the Caribbean—Curacao. Though the population of Curacao is only 160,000—less than the population of the entire city of Providence, Rhode Island—the island has sent 14 players to Major League Baseball since 2014. That's the most players per capita of any country in the world, and doesn't even include the other 25 players on minor league rosters.[1] Baseball has been played on Curacao for 80 years, supposedly traceable to a game between Dominican laborers and Venezuelan fruit sellers. Like in many other Caribbean countries, baseball is one of the most popular sports on the island.

How does all of that explain how the Netherlands won the World Baseball Classic? The answer lies in Curacao's long and complicated colonial history, a story of colonialism repeated with variations around the globe over the last five hundred years. The original inhabitants of

Curacao were the Amerindian Arawaks who had migrated from South America six thousand years ago. Spanish soldier/explorer Alonso de Ojeda, along with Italian Amerigo Vespucci (after whom both North and South America were named), landed on Curacao on a voyage in the early sixteenth century. This brought a wave of Spanish settlement that petered out in the seventeenth century due to the lack of gold and fresh water. By 1634, the Dutch West India Company had laid claim to the island, installing its own governor. During the European wars of the nineteenth century, Curacao was passed back and forth between the British, French, and Dutch before falling into the hands of the Dutch once again. Curacao had once been a center for the Atlantic slave trade, but with the abolition of slavery in the mid-nineteenth century, the island fell on hard times economically. It wasn't until oil was discovered in nearby Venezuela in 1903 that Curacao's fortune changed. Oil refineries were constructed on the island to help process Venezuelan oil.[2]

Like many countries across the globe that had suffered under colonial control, after World War II Curacao joined other Caribbean states in a call for independence from the Netherlands. The Dutch granted the island a measure of autonomy within the larger kingdom, but independence didn't come until 2010. As is the case of nations within the United Kingdom (England, Scotland, Wales, and Northern Ireland), Curacaoans are Dutch citizens with their own separate parliament and prime minister. Most Curacaoans, including former and current MLB players like Andruw Jones and Andrelton Simmons, are taught Dutch in schools, but also learn English and Spanish (partly because of the colonial legacy of those countries' role in Curacaoan history and culture) as well as Papiamentu, a creole language that combines elements of Portuguese, Spanish, Dutch, English, French, African languages, and the language of the original Arawak Indians.[3] Because Curacao remains a constituent country of the Kingdom of the Netherlands, Curacaoan players are eligible to play for the Netherlands during the World Baseball Classic, and that is the very complicated answer to why the Dutch are so good at baseball.

A BRIEF GUIDE TO COLONIALISM

Curacao's story explains why athletes from the island would play for the Kingdom of the Netherlands team. We didn't explain why people from

Venezuela and the Dominican Republic would have brought baseball to the island in the first place. Or why other Caribbean countries like Cuba, the Dominican Republic, and Venezuela also excel in international baseball competitions. To understand those stories, we have to understand exactly what colonialism is. Curacao's history gives us a glimpse into colonialism as a system, which involves the subjugation of one nation by another, conquering its population and then exploiting its economic resources.[4] A succession of European countries took over Curacao and other Caribbean islands explicitly for their usefulness to the colonial power. Colonialism also often involves forcing the language and culture of the colonial power onto its colonized countries. This is why Curacaoans speak Dutch, and have a legal system based on Dutch law. Colonialism as a social, cultural, and economic system dominated the world from the fifteenth century well into the twenty-first century—as we saw, Curacao didn't gain its independence until 2010.

As colonialism dictated the spread of language and culture, it also had an important role to play in global patterns of which sports were played where. One way to trace the influence of European countries on their colonized nations is through the presence of different sports. Cricket is most popular in countries that were once under British colonial control, such as Australia, India, Pakistan, Jamaica, New Zealand, South Africa, and the West Indies. Because of the legacy of British colonial control, the world's most tense sports match is when the Indian and Pakistani national cricket teams play each other. A similar pattern exists for golf, with players from former British colonies often dominating the sport in the mid- to late-twentieth century. Where the United States had influence—in the Caribbean, Central and South America, but also Asia—baseball became a popular sport. Like food, language, and music, sports are one way to trace the complex path of history on a global level.

"IT'S NOT CRICKET": SPORTS AND COLONIAL POWER

Sir Ranjitsinhji Vibhaji is one of the world's greatest cricket players, serving as team captain for the Sussex team in England and scoring 985 runs for England in 15 test matches between England and Australia.[5] He was also an Indian maharaja, or a prince of his native state of Nawanagar, which he ruled from 1907 until his death in 1933. It's no coincidence that an Indian maharaja was also an outstanding cricket player. Sports were one tool used by the British to maintain their colonial control in places like India. Often known as Ranji, Sir Vibhaji learned cricket at Rajkumar College, an institution set up by the British to educate Indian princes. He spent hours every day practicing cricket under the eye of an English coach, becoming a model for what was "possible" for Indians under British control.[6]

Cricket and other sports helped the British maintain control by convincing colonized peoples that British culture was superior and worthy of being imitated. In the case of the British in India, at its largest, the Indian Civil Service was made up of only about eleven hundred men. That means about a thousand British civil servants controlled a vast continent of over 200 million people. There were standing armies as well, but those armies were composed mostly of native Indians.[7] How does a very small group of people control a much larger population? Partly by establishing cultural hegemony, or persuading Indians that British language, customs, and institutions were superior to those of India. That was no easy task, given the thousands of years of rich and sophisticated Indian culture and history. Sports had an important part to play in this larger colonial project, and these were spread through two institutions—schools and the church.

Schools established by the British or that were under British influence throughout their empire included an education in British sports, especially cricket and rugby union.[8] The rationales for teaching colonial subjects to play cricket and rugby were similar to the dynamics discussed in chapter 6 that shaped sports as a masculine domain. Just as sport would ensure that American men remain masculine and that workers would learn to take orders from authority figures like coaches and managers, cricket and rugby in places like India would mold the natives into models of British masculinity, willing to take up their place in the complicated bureaucracy that was British rule. Sports were a way to create the kind of colonial subjects who would be easiest to control. To play and understand cricket was as much about being honest, upright, and accepting conformity as it was about taking part in a game.[9] Hence, the common British expression, "It's not cricket," an idiom that implies something is not fair, sportsmanlike, or legitimate.[10] Lord Harris, British governor of Bombay (now Mumbai) and cricket coach, was of the opinion that select groups of Indians would be ready for political responsibility only after they had assimilated the playing and behavioral codes of cricket.[11] Once sports like cricket and rugby were established, their governance echoed that of the colonial power system. Disputes about rules were referred back to organizing bodies in England, rather than being decided by native groups. Rule books and manuals of style dictating how the games were to be played were written by British men. Initially, at least, Britain as the colonial power had ultimate authority over exactly how the games should be played.[12]

Sports were also spread through missionary work and the ideals of muscular Christianity. Muscular Christianity was a philosophical movement of nineteenth-century British life, which associated physical activity with the civilizing properties of Christianity. It was connected to a fear of feminization among men and boys in religious spheres, and sought to correct that with an emphasis on sports. It's not surprising, then, that many missionaries brought sports with them to their colonial outposts. Reverend Greville John Chester, for example, argued in the 1860s that poor West Indian black youths needed to learn cricket.[13] To teach West Indians how to play cricket, then, was to teach them how to become British subjects—literally people under the control of British power.

To point out the ways in which sports were a tool of colonial control doesn't mean that sometimes the influence didn't go the other way. Certainly, the British and other colonial powers brought their own sports culture with them to their colonized subjects. But they also learned and adapted native sports, like polo. Polo is an ancient game, dating back as early as the sixth century BCE in the Persian empire. The British discovered the game being played in the Himalayan hill states of India and called it "polo" after the Balti word for "ball."[14] The original game had no goals, no teams, no restrictions on the number of players, and no physical boundaries. Twenty years later, the game had been completely transformed by the British military establishment, with a prescribed field of play, rules, and a set number of players with designated roles and positions. The British version of polo included recognized tactics written up in manuals (by British men) and emphasized the importance of good equipment and horses. The sport became a useful tool of the British military, played mostly at military stations and eventually adopted by Indian princes like Ranji.

It's also important to note that the spread of sport to colonized people wasn't always an intentional, top-down process. In some cases, colonial powers made explicit links between sport and controlling natives. But in many colonized countries, internal divisions that existed before colonial control also drove their adaption of sports. A common tool of colonial domination was to pit ethnic, caste, or social class groups against each other. In other words, colonial rulers employed a strategy of divide and conquer. In the case of sports like polo and golf, access was at first given only to certain groups, designated as worthy and capable of becoming "civilized," that is, British. Polo, for example, was seen by Indian princes as a way to demonstrate their affinity for British imperial power, but also fit their traditional and continuing cultural role—which was to demonstrate lavish wealth to their subjects. Polo, an expensive sport, was an attractive means to continue that tradition.

THE FORT SHAW WOMEN'S BASKETBALL TEAM: NATIVE AMERICAN SPORT AND INTERNAL COLONIALISM

In places like India and the West Indies, colonial powers used sports as a means to both control and assimilate their subjects. Assimilation refers to the process by which one group adopts the cultural practices of another and gives up their own. Assimilation is both a description of reality and an ideal. That is, in places like the United States, immigrant groups assimilate over time so that by the third generation (the grandchildren of the first people to immigrate), group members usually speak only English, having lost the language of their grandparents altogether. As an ideal, assimilation is something that is often forced on people, willing or not, as a means to control and dominate. One example of assimilation by force in the United States is the case of Native Americans—an example of internal colonialism—and this experience had an effect on the games they played, as well as who played them.

Before Europeans showed up in North America, women played an active role in many aspects of Native American tribal life, including games and sporting activities. Unlike the prevailing views among Europeans at the time, among many tribes there was no perception that sports and games were for men and not women. Physical strength wasn't seen as "unfeminine" and, in fact, the strongest women made the best mothers and homemakers. Native American women enjoyed sports that required strength and skill just as much as men, and their games were often highly competitive.[15]

Because Native American culture changed so drastically after contact with Europeans, it's hard to precisely re-create women's sporting lives prior to European arrival. But the evidence we have suggests women across tribes engaged in a wide range of sports and games. Among both the Navajo and Apache, running was an important element in initiation rites for girls. A young Navajo girl would engage in a four-day initiation rite, running up to three times a day, each time longer than the last. The longer distance she ran, the stronger her strength of character and her bravery were. Distances were also believed to increase her chances to acquire sheep, horses, and children. Among some tribes of the Southwest, running might be combined with pushing a ball or a piece of wood. Other tribes emphasized swimming or wrestling.[16]

The sports and games played by Native American women were often still gender-segregated, even though they were likely to be similar to activities engaged in by men. Among the Choctaw, women played their own version of a stickball game. Like modern lacrosse (which evolved from Native American games), players used forked branches or two sticks to catch a ball. In the women's game, the ball was made of two deerskin bags, tied together by a leather strap. This double ball game allowed women to play a high-contact, competitive sport like the men while still maintaining a symbolic distance from the masculine world. The game also hinted at an inversion of the gender order, as the game was called "the testicle game" by the women in reference to the shape of the bag.[17]

With extended European contact, the sport and games of Native Americans, along with most aspects of their culture, disappeared. This was partly due to the decimation of Native American populations as a result of disease and violence. But the U.S. government and religious authorities also pursued policies of forced assimilation in order to deprive Native Americans of their land. Many Native American children were sent to boarding schools and federal schools where the curriculum emphasized adopting white European culture and abandoning any traces of their native culture. In a dynamic similar to that in places like India and the West Indies, sports were part of this process of attempting to assimilate Native Americans to white culture. But part of that white culture was an association of sports with masculinity. The rich game and sporting culture among Native American women was mostly erased in these schools. To encourage Native American women to play sports was seen by white officials as encouraging their uncontrollable and unsociable character.[18] So their exposure to European culture reduced Native American women's access to sports and games.

One exception to this general trend happened at Fort Shaw, a Native American boarding school in Montana. Three recent graduates from another Native American boarding school, including Josephine Langley, were invited to join the staff at Fort Shaw as teaching assistants. Perhaps it was Langley's status as Native American herself (she was a Piegan Indian) that led her to teach basketball to girls at the school. By 1897, Fort Shaw was the only school at any level—high school or college—that incorporated basketball into its physical curriculum. The following year, Langley formed a women's basketball team and by 1903 they had clinched the Montana state title and transformed basketball into the most exciting spectator sport in the state. In 1904, the team was invited to the St. Louis World's Fair, where they amused visitors with concerts, sporting demonstrations, reading activities, and other programs. The Fort Shaw school was shut down in 1910, but the Fort Shaw "Blues," as the women's team was known, was instrumental in creating a style of basketball known as "Rezball," or the style of basketball played by Native Americans on reservations. The term is still used to describe a particularly Native American type of play, characterized by quick shots and an aggressive defense that puts pressure on players on all parts of the court.[19] These Native American women were instrumental in taking a white man's sport and making it their own.

BEATING THEM AT THEIR OWN GAME

In spite of attempts to control the rules and style of play, as sports spread through colonial countries, changes did occur. Take the example of the Trobriand Islands, where missionaries hoped to use cricket to curb the tribal warfare of the indigenous peoples. Trobrianders embraced cricket, but changed the game to suit their own cultural norms. Instead of bowling overarm in the British fashion, Trobrianders delivered the ball using their traditional spear-throwing actions. They allowed any number of players to compete, as long as the numbers of the team were even. Tribal markings and dances were made part of the ritual of play. Matches became a focal point of village political activity and the home side was always allowed to win, though not by too many points, in order not to cause offense to the away team. Cricket for the Trobrianders became, not a tool of colonial oppression, but a way to maintain their own culture.[20]

All over the colonized world similar adaptations and alterations took place. In New Zealand, the rugby union team the All Blacks have become famous for their performance of a traditional Maori dance before each game. The *haka* dance, has come to be associated with New Zealand national pride, though initially rugby was used in New Zealand in ways similar to cricket in India—to "civilize" the natives.[21] Now the *haka*, once seen as a signal of the Maori's lack of civilization, has become an important sport ritual.

Eventually, colonial subjects were able not just to make the games their own, but to beat their colonial masters. This was always a flaw in the strategy of using sports as a measure of the progress toward "civilization" among colonized peoples. When they were finally able to outperform their supposed "betters," it provided fuel to the argument that equality had been achieved and colonial rule was no longer necessary. As the twentieth century progressed and more colonized countries began demanding independence, their sports victories against colonial powers added fuel to their arguments. In India, the Mohan Bagan cricket team defeated the East Yorkshire Regiment (an English team) in 1911 and the victory was widely regarded as a sign of Indian development, equality, and even superiority.[22] One Bengali-language newspaper wrote of the victory:

> It fills every Indian with pride and joy to know that rice-eating, malaria-ridden, bare-footed Bengalis have got the better of beef-eating, Herculean, booted John Bull in that peculiarly English sport.[23]

This victory did much to help Bengalis overcome their sense of physical and cultural inferiority. On the other side of the globe, West Indians celebrated in 1950 when their team won its first cricket test match on English soil, composing songs about their black cricket heroes, while Australia and New Zealand also celebrated rugby union victories against England. Just as sport had played a role in the subjugation of colonial countries, it also became a part of movements to throw off colonial oppression.

THE LAST "AFRICAN" WORLD CUP TEAM

In today's world, regardless of which sport you watch, part of what you're seeing on the field or the court is the continuing legacy of colonialism, as well as more modern forces of globalization. The imperial ambitions of the United States came later than those of European countries, but those aspirations are still evident on American playing fields. This is especially true on the baseball diamond. Baseball certainly has its origins in the United States, but it's not the only country that can lay claim to a long and rich tradition with the sport. Most trace the development of baseball in the United States to the post–Civil War era. But as early as the 1860s, Cubans were taking to baseball enthusiastically. The sport was brought to the island by young men who had attended school in the United States. During this period of unrest and strife on the island as Cubans fought for independence from Spain, elite Cubans were able to travel easily back and forth to the United States. Many parents sent their children to U.S. schools as an escape from chaotic conditions in Cuba. It was one of these young men, Esteban Bellán, who started the first professional league in Cuba.[24] It formed in 1870, just one year after the first professional game was played in the United States.[25] Mexicans began playing around the same time, challenging North American sailors and railroad workers to games. In the same time period, baseball was being played in Hawaii and Japan.[26]

By the early twentieth century, baseball was being explicitly tied to America's imperial ambitions. A. G. Spalding was one of American baseball's earliest stars and entrepreneurs (his sporting goods store became the Spalding company, still responsible for the manufacture of many types of sporting equipment). On the topic of baseball's spread, Spalding proclaimed in 1910 that the function of baseball was to "follow the flag around the world."[27] Spalding paired baseball with the American idea of manifest destiny, that the United States had a divine right to spread across the North American continent and around the world. Spalding went so far as to declare, "baseball is war!" by tracing the way it spread to the Philippines, Puerto Rico, and Cuba (all places where the U.S. military had been engaged).[28] These long histories with the sport are part of what explain the large number of Latino and Asian players in Major League Baseball today, where Hispanic players make up 27 percent of the league and 29 percent of players were born outside the United States.[29]

In the soccer world, the victorious men's French World Cup team was celebrated for its ethnic diversity. Players hail from all over the world, like striker Kylian Mbappé, born in France to a Cameroonian father and an Algerian mother. Or midfielder Paul Pogba, whose parents are Guinean.[30] Only two players on the 2018 team laid claim to strong, ancestral roots in France going back multiple generations. The presence of players of African origin on the team was so strong that some commentators referred to the French team as the last surviving "African" team in the tournament.[31]

The preponderance of French players of African origins on the World Cup team is a relic of France's own colonial history as well as a result of globalization. It's no coincidence that many of the players hail from African countries that were once French colonies or under French influence, like Cameroon and Algeria. Coming from these French-speaking countries makes immigrating to France an easier transition. Thus, the paths of current immigration often still run along the grooves laid down by colonial pasts.

GLOBALIZATION, IMMIGRATION, AND SPORT

The immigration of people from formerly colonized countries to the countries that were once colonial powers is one piece of the larger picture of globalization. Globalization in general is the way that money, people, technology, culture, and power are increasingly interconnected, circulating around the world in complicated patterns. Globalization is often thought of as a more recent process, though all of those things—money, people, technology, culture, and power—have been moving around for a long time. It might be accurate to say that they all move a lot faster in today's world with the aid of the internet and airplanes.

The movement of people, specifically, causes a great deal of tension and conflict all over the world. For example, though the 2018 French team was celebrated after their victory, in 2011 French soccer leaders suggested that the number of soccer players with dual nationalities (like Mbappé and Pogba) should be capped in the country's elite soccer academies. In effect, they were suggesting that a limit be placed on the number of players having African origins who would be able to play at elite levels, such as the national team. The suggestion originated out of a desire to preserve "our culture, our history," by which these officials meant the history of people of French descent for generations rather than the more recent African immigrants.

All over Europe, immigrants from former colonized countries face hostility, on and off the soccer pitch. Linton Harris, an English player of African descent, is just one in a long line of players to be subjected to racist taunts, including monkey noises.[32] Trailblazing black soccer players in the 1970s and 1980s had to endure monkey noises as well as bananas being thrown at them on the field. When Harris was sent off the field in a 2019 match, someone shouted from the crowd, "Typical black man, ruining the game."[33] A player who supported Harris by arguing with the referee was then also sent off. To protest, the entire team then walked off the pitch and the game was abandoned. Reports of racist abuse in soccer—on and off the field—seem to be on the rise. It's unclear whether the explanation lies in an actual increase in racist behavior, or the younger generation of players have become more vocal about the discrimination they face.

On the baseball field in the United States, anti-immigration sentiment might be more subtle, but there's still not equality between native white players and their Latino counterparts. Native-born American players and foreign-born Latino players enter the league through two separate and unequal systems. American players go through a national draft system, with certain guaranteed income levels and eligibility only after they've graduated from high school. Latino players are recruited by scouts in a lawless free-for-all which some legal scholars have suggested might involve serious violations of international labor laws as well as the exploitation of Third World children.[34]

Take the case of Laumin Bessa, a young Venezuelan prospect recruited by the Cleveland Indians in 1998. The Indians scout, Luis Aponte, signed Bessa, who was 15 years old at the time. Aponte then hid Bessa until he reached the age of 16, when he was legally eligible to sign according to MLB rules. Though Bessa's signing bonus was $300,000, his family only received $30,000, because Aponte had apportioned the money, doling it out contingent on Bessa meeting certain criteria for development set by the Indians. Aponte's actions violated MLB rules in that he both signed an underage player and divided up his signing bonus. When the violations came to the attention of the baseball commissioner, Cleveland drew a fine and other minor sanctions.[35]

This lax enforcement of rules in Latino countries has resulted in what some baseball critics call a "boatload mentality" in the MLB.[36] In 2001, the Cleveland Indians spent $700,000 to sign 40 Latin American prospects, while Cleveland's top pick in the draft for American-born players received almost $1.7 million. Teams can get a "boatload" of Dominican or Venezuelan players for the same price as one American-born player. Young boys and men from these countries are treated as commodities, "a boatload of cheap Dominicans, as if these human beings were pieces of exported fruit."[37] In this particular baseball dynamic, the history of colonialism as a system of exploitation is re-created.

THE BAT FLIP AND STYLES OF PLAY

When Latino players make it into the league, their style of play is often criticized as not lining up with "American" baseball norms. As we discussed with cricket in the Trobriand Islands, baseball as it's played in the Caribbean and Latin America looks very different than a typical MLB game in the United States. In countries like the Dominican Republic, an alternative baseball culture and style emerged. Games played in the Dominican Republic are loud and raucous affairs among both the fans and the players when compared to American games. The fans play music throughout the game. The style of play emphasizes hustle and baseball smartness over the athletic power given precedence in the United States. Thus, Roger Maris, an eventual Hall of Fame player in the MLB, was cut from a Dominican team because he didn't demonstrate the necessary hustle. This emphasis on hustle means that though there are Latino power hitters, the preference is for line drives and speed in base running. Dominican shortstops are more likely to one-hand the ball over the two-handed style taught in the United States. Trick play in general is an essential part of the game in the Dominican Republic, while it's generally frowned upon in the United States.[38]

In places like the Dominican Republic, baseball is played with style and flare. Bat flips are common. When a player hits a home run, he's likely to throw his bat into the air so that it flips end over end as a celebration of his achievement. Hitting a home run is no easy thing in a game where the very best batters only hit the ball successfully four out of ten times. But the norms of American baseball dictate that players be stoic and workmanlike. Celebrations of almost any sort are frowned upon. Hence, Latino players get criticized for flipping their bats. Cuban player Yasiel Puig is constantly criticized in the media for his exuberance as a player, being sent down to the minor leagues despite playing a critical role in his team getting to the World Series in 2017. The end result is that though Americans sometimes forcefully spread the sport of baseball around the world, they are less than accepting of the form of the sport that comes back to them as played by Latino players. Rather than accept and celebrate the diversity of baseball culture in places like the Dominican Republic, many major leaguers insist that Latino players assimilate to American norms of what white, working-class baseball should look like.

GLOBALIZATION AND SPORTS TODAY

At the same time many baseball commentators criticize the playing style of Latin Americans, in 2019, Major League Baseball played four regular season games in Mexico as rumors spread that Mexico City could be the location for the league's next expansion team.[39] In 2016, the MLB opened offices in Mexico City and has steadily increased its presence through both spring training and regular season games. The National Football League will also play one of its regular season games in Mexico as well as four games in London as part of its NFL International Series.[40] In 2019 the National Basketball Association played its ninth regular-season game in London. Why are these leagues seeking to expand beyond North America?

Soccer has long been called the world's game, and now other sports are trying to compete for that status. The MLB, NFL, and NBA are all expanding overseas in order to increase the global market for their game. Unlike in the colonial era, the goal is no longer to make fans all over the world into docile subjects for colonial control. Or at least, that's not explicitly the goal. These leagues want more fans in order to increase their profits. Selling NFL jerseys and television rights to people in the United States isn't enough. Like other corporations and organizations in the age of globalization, sports, too, face pressure to expand outside of national boundaries. Looking at the NBA specifically, the global audience has been its fastest growing market.[41] Basketball has been especially successful catching on in China, one of the biggest markets available. Over 300 million people in China play basketball, with double that number watching NBA programming on TV.[42]

Like the Olympic movement, this contemporary globalization has the potential to connect people in new and positive ways. Fans all over the world can now cheer for Manchester United or the Boston Celtics. Global sports certainly have the potential to bring us together. But as we've seen, the old power dynamics that were created during the colonial era haven't disappeared. Many critics of globalization argue that it constitutes a new form of colonialism where power and control are achieved through financial domination rather than outright political control.

8

THE BEST ITALIAN BASEBALL PLAYER IS BLACK

How the Histories of Sport and Race Intertwine

The famous biologist and baseball fan, Stephen Jay Gould, had a favorite sports trivia question: "Which Italian American player for the Brooklyn Dodgers once hit 40 home runs in a season?" It was Gould's favorite because the way it stumps many people reveals an interesting facet of American ideas about race. Roy Campanella hit 40 home runs for the Dodgers, but most people consider Campanella to be black rather than Italian American, even though his father was Italian American. The "one-drop rule" in American racial classification systems means that Campanella's Italian ancestry is generally ignored in favor of his African American background. The same thing is true of Tiger Woods (who has black, Filipino, Native American, and white ancestry) and President Barack Obama (who has a white mother and an African father). The one-drop rule means that a single drop of African American blood classifies a person as black, regardless of the rest of their racial ancestry. The case of Roy Campanella is just one story in the fascinating history of how ideas about race and sports intertwine.

BEFORE JACKIE ROBINSON:
MOSES FLEETWOOD WALKER

When people in the United States think of race and sports, Jackie Robinson might be the figure most likely to come to mind. In 1947—seven years before the landmark *Brown v. Board of Education* decision which made segregation illegal, and eight years before Rosa Parks refused to move to the back of the bus as part of the larger Montgomery bus boycott—Robinson broke the color line in baseball. The story of the prejudice Robinson faced, with some teams being encouraged by their managers to chant racial slurs at Robinson, is familiar to most Americans.[1] In today's Major League Baseball, Jackie Robinson is honored on April 15, the day he first took the field for the Los Angeles Dodgers, and every player wears his number.

The question that doesn't get asked very often is, how did professional baseball become segregated in the first place? As with the system of Jim Crow segregation that took shape in the South following the Civil War, the exclusion of black players from baseball wasn't an inevitable outcome. It has a specific history that begins with Moses Fleetwood Walker in 1887. That was the year future Hall of Famer Adrian "Cap" Anson refused to allow his team to play against the Newark team unless Walker and fellow African American player George Stovey were benched. Anson wrote the following letter to the Newark team:

> Dear Sir:
>
> We the undersigned, do hereby warn you not to put up Walker, the Negro catcher, the days you play in Richmond, as we could mention the names of seventy-five determined men who have sworn to mob Walker, if he comes on the grounds in a suit. We hope you will listen to our words of warning, so there will be no trouble, and if you do not, there certainly will be. We only write this to prevent bloodshed, as you alone can prevent.[2]

The manager of Walker's team refused to concede to that demand, but Walker faced continuing harassment and threats of violence. When a Toronto manager asked Walker to leave the stadium, he was supposedly surrounded by fans while brandishing a revolver, threatening to put a hole in someone in the crowd. Walker persisted in the majors until 1889, earning a footnote in history as the last African American player in the league until Jackie Robinson broke the color line 58 years later.

THE JOCKEY SYNDROME

Baseball wasn't the only sport that drove out African Americans. In the nineteenth century, horse racing was probably the most popular sport around, and it was dominated by black jockeys. When the very first Kentucky Derby was run in 1875, 14 out of the 15 jockeys were black. Being a jockey was seen as a "slave job" by whites. Before the abolition of slavery, African American men had ridden horses for their owners. After abolition, it made sense for black jockeys to continue riding and so there was no attempt to challenge black dominance of the sport. When black jockey Isaac Murphy dominated the sport in the 1880s, most of his fellow jockeys were black. Murphy rode in 11 Kentucky Derby races, winning three times.[3] At the peak of his career, he earned $15,000–$20,000 per year, mind-boggling figures for the time period.[4] With that much money to be made in the sport, the white establishment decided the race of jockeys should change. Murphy was run out of the sport, along with other black jockeys, by a combination of three tactics. The first tactic was the formation of Jockey Clubs across the sport, which served as unions for riders. As was true in many other types of unions in the United States, African Americans were exclude from Jockey Clubs. Second, owners themselves stopped hiring black jockeys to ride their horses. Finally, when black jockeys did make it into a race, white jockeys would gang up on them. They'd either trap the black jockey's horse along the rails or between two horses, bump or knock him out of the saddle or, if those tactics didn't work, simply run the horse off the track.[5]

The "jockey syndrome" is one way to describe this phenomenon—the way existing rules are changed in order to maintain control in the face of challenges to white supremacy.[6] The history of African Americans in sports in the United States very much follows this pattern. In boxing, Jack Johnson is the oft-forgotten first black heavyweight champion of the world. Johnson fought for six years to get a shot at a title match against the white champion, bursting his way through the color line in boxing. He won the championship in 1908, creating a serious racial crisis in the boxing world and beyond, spurring the search for the "great white hope," a white boxer who could defeat Johnson. When it became clear Johnson couldn't be defeated inside the ring, he was targeted for his personal life instead. Federal prosecutors accused Johnson of violating the Mann Act, a law that made it illegal to transport women across state lines "for the purpose of prostitution or debauchery, or for any other immoral purpose."[7] The act was meant to prevent "white slavery," but was used to prosecute Johnson, who had a series of white women as romantic partners and wives. Johnson was convicted under the Mann Act in 1913. Rather than serving jail time, he skipped bail and fled to Canada, escaping imprisonment but effectively ending his boxing career.[8] Consistent with jockey syndrome, when the boxing establishment couldn't force Johnson out within the existing rules, they found other means that allowed white control of the sport to continue. It would be another 20 years before another black heavyweight—Joe Louis—took the title again.

JESSE OWENS AND THE EXTINCTION HYPOTHESIS

One of the reasons Jack Johnson's success as a boxer was so revolutionary was because of the way it contradicted the scientific wisdom of the time period regarding race. Take the example of Jesse Owens, the African American runner whose triumph at the 1936 Berlin Olympics was upheld as a victory over Adolf Hitler's fascism and ideas of racial purity. The actual story is more complicated. Owens was born to a family of sharecroppers in Alabama. His family's poverty and lack of access to adequate health care resulted in him losing several siblings to early death. Owens himself was sickly, and the teacher who recommended he try out for track did so not "because he saw any potential champion in me; it was because he saw a potential corpse."[9]

In fact, during the late nineteenth and early twentieth centuries, the prevailing racial science didn't emphasize the physical superiority of African Americans. Instead it predicted that inherent differences among black people in the United States would lead to their decreasing vitality and eventual demise. Statistician Frederick Hoffman concluded in his famous essay, "Race, Traits and Tendencies of the American Negro," that according to his extinction hypothesis, the eventual disappearance of African Americans as a race was coded into their very DNA. He based his conclusions on real statistical data about the rates of disease and mortality among African Americans during the time period, but ignored the social and economic sources of these racial differences. [10]

With the wave of success achieved by Jesse Owens and other African American athletes during the time period, racial scientists re-examined their previous notions. Jesse Owens's body was picked apart for a physical explanation of black athletic superiority, as scientists once again ignored the role of culture, history, or circumstance. The sole dissenting voice in the rush to conclude that African Americans were genetically superior athletes was black anthropologist and physician Montague Cobb. Cobb looked at Owens's feet, his legs, his calves, and his chest capacity before concluding that it was impossible to attribute Owens's amazing ability to his race. As Cobb wrote, "There is not one, single, physical feature, including skin color, which all our Negro champions have in common which would identify them as Negro." [11] In other words, the problem with trying to identify a physical or genetic component that makes African Americans better athletes is that there is no physical or genetic reality to the category itself. Race is a social category, not a biological or genetic one, as anthropologists, biologists, and geneticists have definitively proven. As Cobb pointed out, among the people identified as "Negro athletes," none of them all had the same skin color, hair type, facial features, height, foot size or shape, calves, legs, or other features. What the most sophisticated current techniques tell us about racial groupings is that any two people in two different so-called races are as likely to be more genetically similar to each other than two people in the same so-called race. That is, if you are classified as Asian, you're no more likely to be genetically similar to another Asian person than you are to someone classified as African American. [12]

That race has no biological underpinnings that would explain athletic ability might seem difficult to believe until you think about the contradictions of racial categories in the first place. Take the category of Asian American. This category includes people of Chinese, Japanese, and Korean descent, but also those from the Indian subcontinent. Why should we expect people from Bangladesh or Pakistan to be more genetically similar to those from China or Japan? If we look at the history of racial categories as defined by the U.S. Census, the way in which race is measured has changed every time from 1790 until 2000. That is, for every 10-year period, the Census defined race differently, meaning that a person could go from being a mulatto (at least half African American mixed with white ancestry) in 1920 to being Negro in 1930, as the categories shifted.[13] Because different countries and cultures have different systems of racial classification, it's also possible to change races when traveling from one place to another.

WHY IS THE CENTER ALWAYS WHITE? RACE AND STACKING

Race as a biological category isn't real. We look different from each other, but those physical differences don't line up along racial lines. You can't tell by looking at someone what their ethnic background is. Just ask anyone who's had their ethnicity constantly misattributed. Those physical differences (skin color, hair form, facial features, etc.) also don't line up with deeper traits, like intelligence or athletic ability. Nonetheless, sports are an important area where beliefs about the biological nature of race are reinforced. Even in the twenty-first century, people continue to search for a biological component to the dominance of one race or ethnic group in a particular sport. For example, in 2000 Jon Entine sparked controversy when he published a book arguing that black athletes have a biological advantage, while scholarly articles that seek to verify some essential difference continue to appear.[14] These beliefs reinforce the common notion of race as a biological category, giving strength to the idea that people in different racial groups are inherently different and, often, superior or inferior to others.

The repercussions of believing that one racial or ethnic group could be better at golf or basketball or curling might not at first seem to be particularly damaging. After all, a belief in the biological superiority of African Americans in sports like basketball is about their *superiority*—ways in which they're *better* than some other group. But these beliefs are part of a larger ideology that holds that if African Americans or other groups are athletically superior, they're *inferior* in other areas, like intelligence and leadership ability.

The way in which ideas about athletic superiority and inferiority are paired can be seen in the phenomenon of *stacking*, or position allocation. Stacking refers to minority players being relegated to certain team positions and excluded from competing for others.[15] In other words, positions on the playing field are often racially segregated in ways that mirror wider society. African American players tend to be stacked in positions that match the existing stereotypes about their physical superiority, while white players are more likely to be in the positions that are seen as requiring intelligence and leadership or that have greater outcome control. In baseball, the positions of pitcher, catcher, and center fielder are less racially stacked than in the past, but it's still true that only seven African American pitchers have ever started at the All-Star Game in that event's 90-year history.[16] In softball, it's still rare to see an African American woman on the pitcher's mound.[17]

The NFL provides a particularly striking example of stacking, where often the "whitest" positions are those up the middle of the field. On offense, those positions include quarterbacks and centers. Doug Williams, as the first black quarterback to guide a team to the Super Bowl in 1988, paved the way for a new generation of African American men in the position. Still, Warren Moon is the only black quarterback in the NFL Hall of Fame, and he had to fight to be able to play the position at the professional level. Tracking the percentage of African American quarterbacks from 1999 to 2014, the numbers increased only from 18 to 19 percent, and those black quarterbacks in the league are more likely to be benched than their white counterparts.[18] While across all positions, black players make up 74 percent of the league, only 18 percent of centers are African American.[19] At corner back, a position believed to require natural speed and athletic ability, there are currently no white players in the NFL and haven't been any since 2003.[20]

Stacking has important repercussions beyond just creating a system of secondary segregation on the field. The effects of stacking filter up through the leadership ranks in the NFL, having repercussions for entrance into coaching. It makes sense that when teams look to hire coaches, they look first to the positions on the field that are most associated with intelligence, leadership, and control of the game. Because those players are disproportionately white, the field of potential coaching candidates underrepresents black players. In addition, until recently, former-players-turned-coaches tended to come from the offensive rather than the defensive side of the field and, across the NFL, 80 percent of the defensive players are black.[21] In addition, the positions into which white players are segregated are often also the positions with lower rates of injury, which may create a context in which physical harm to black players is taken less seriously than that to white athletes.[22]

What explains the persistence of stacking? Like many forms of discrimination, positional allocation doesn't make rational sense. If, as a
coach, you select only from white players to be your center, you're going
to miss out on the many African American players who may excel at that
position. Coaches and managers aren't explicitly thinking to themselves
that black athletes can't be centers. The process is more subtle, and has to
do with category selection. When a coach or manager thinks about who
they want at the center or corner back position, they might imagine in
their head a prototypical player at that position. Perhaps at center they
want a player like Jason Kelce, who is white, and a corner back like
Patrick Peterson, who is black. As coaches evaluate players in the draft,
race is one of the factors that correlates. So coaches and managers looking for a center like Jason Kelce will focus only on white players, while
those looking for a corner back like Patrick Peterson will only consider
black players.[23] There's clear evidence for this dynamic in the way sports
commentators talk about players, almost always making comparisons
within rather than across racial categories. Though there are white quarterbacks who have a scrambling style of play similar to Cam Newton,
black quarterbacks like Newton are hardly ever compared to white quarterbacks.[24] Wes Welker, a white slot receiver, is always compared to
other white players, sometimes even though those players didn't play at
the same position as Welker. He's never compared to other short, speedy
slot receivers who are African American.[25] This focus on categories and
positional prototypes rather than an analysis of individuals means that
NFL coaches and managers go on re-creating racial segregation by position.

INVINCIBLE BODIES: RACIALIZATION AND SPORT

The ways in which sports commentators compare only within racial categories rather than across them is just one example of how sports media
contribute to racial stereotypes. Repeated studies have found racial bias in
sports coverage, mostly centered around themes of "black brawn vs.
white brains." In these narratives, black players are described as "naturally gifted" or possessing "God-given talent," while white players have a
"mind for the game" and are "disciplined."[26] Commentators and sports-
writers emphasize the intelligence and work ethic of white players as

opposed to the natural abilities of black athletes. The same dynamics have been found to extend into recruiting and scouting, where reports of black athletes emphasize their physical talents while white athletes are described in positive mental terms. In this way, black versus white is mirrored by the dichotomy of physical versus mental, or body versus mind. White players become a sort of everyman, scrappily overcoming physical deficit in natural athletic ability through determination and grit. There are also differences in how emotion on the field is viewed for white and black players. When white players lash out on the field, they're described as having "moxie" and being passionate leaders who inspire their team. Their emotions are praised, and when they trash-talk or get into trouble off the field, they're more likely to be given a second chance compared to black players.[27]

The different narratives surrounding black and white athletes have important implications beyond just seeing one group as more athletic and the other as smarter. One study sought to discover whether different types of praise had subtly dehumanizing effects. The researchers found that bodily focused praise correlated with believing that athletes have lower capacities for self-control, thinking, and expressing emotions. Praising athletes primarily for their physical abilities was also related to having less support for those athletes' rights to things like unionization and medical coverage for their injuries.[28]

Sports, then, becomes part of the process of racialization, or the way racial meaning is ascribed to a social practice or a group. In sports, white bodies are normalized and humanized, while black bodies are dehumanized and othered. When a group is dehumanized, it simply means that humanity is denied to those people. Empathy with people within that group is reduced. One result is a desensitization to pain, injury, and violence as experienced by this group. Studies have shown that whites both react differently to images of black people in pain, and assume that black people feel less pain do than white people.[29] Sports, where black athletes are seen as more physically than mentally gifted, contributes to this overall dehumanization. In one study, researchers found that when sports commentators talked about injuries to black college football players, they relied on a narrative of the young men as inhuman and invulnerable. For example, commentators would discuss the injury histories of white players, expressing admiration and praise when they returned to the field after being hurt. The history of black players' injuries was much less likely to be discussed, and the return of a black player to the field after being hurt was taken for granted.

HAIR AND NAILS: THE STRUGGLES OF AFRICAN AMERICAN WOMEN IN SPORTS

Because they sit at the intersection of at least two systems of oppression—race and gender—African American female athletes face their own unique set of challenges in the sports world. They battle a wide range of assumptions and stigmas, sometimes coming under fire from the black community for competing in traditionally white sports while also facing death threats from whites for encroaching on previously segregated territory, like fairways and tennis courts.[30] Unlike their male counterparts, much of the discrimination faced by black women centers on their appearance. When African American gymnast Gabby Douglas made Olympic history in 2012 by becoming the first American gymnast to win gold in both the individual all-around and the team competitions, much of the conversation online and in the media focused on her hair. Douglas's natural hair was referred to as unkempt and unsightly, often by other black women. In the 2016 Olympics in Rio, she faced yet another round of criticism.[31]

Douglas is just the latest in a long line of black women athletes whose accomplishments are often ignored in favor of an emphasis on appearance. Track and field star Florence Griffith Joyner was discussed as much for her fashion choices—her nails, her hair, and her famous one-legged running suits—as she was for her athletic abilities. Coverage of both Venus and Serena Williams often emphasizes what they're wearing or how their hair is done over their impressive victories. Stories about Olympic gold medalist swimmer Simone Manuel focused on how black women's hair serves as a barrier to swimming.[32] Olympic fencer Ibtihaj Muhammad, who is both African American and a practicing Muslim, received death threats and hostility from her teammates because she wears the hijab (modest dress that varies from a head scarf to full body coverage, worn by many Muslim women) while competing.[33]

These added concerns about appearance make it difficult for black women athletes to negotiate their sport as well as their public image. When African American shot putter, Michelle Carter, was told she was going to be featured in publicity material for the upcoming Olympics, she immediately thought about how to make her image as a black woman more appealing, which included straightening her hair. Softball player A. J. Andrews was the first woman to win a Rawlings Golden Glove Award but has no softball glove named after her, unlike many other white female softball players.[34] The pressure on black women athletes to monitor their appearance affects their ability to get endorsements and make money playing the sport they love.

THE RISE AND FALL OF JEWISH BASKETBALL

Members of certain racial or ethnic groups don't end up in a particular sport or playing a particular position on the field because of any underlying biological or genetic reasons. How, then, do certain racial and ethnic groups come to dominate certain sports? As we saw in chapter 7, part of the explanation has to do with the long history of colonialism and current patterns of globalization. If you didn't grow up in Ireland, watching and playing that country's most popular sport of hurling, it's unlikely that you're going to excel in that particular sport. A particular ethnic group can't come to dominate a sport unless they're first exposed to it.

In the United States, successive waves of immigrants have left their traces on the history of various sports. Today, basketball at the professional level is dominated by African American players, who make up 80.7 percent of the NBA.[35] Films such as *White Men Can't Jump* reflect the belief that this dominance is based in essential biological differences. In fact, the explanation lies more in the types of environments where basketball is most likely to be played—urban environments—along with the long history of institutionalized racial segregation. Simply put, basketball courts take up a lot less space than football, baseball, or soccer fields. It's also a fairly cheap sport to play. If you have a court, all you need are a ball and a pair of shoes. It makes sense, then, that when certain racial or ethnic groups are forced into dense, urban settings, they are more likely to take up the sport.[36]

In the twenty-first century, that means African Americans, but in the first half of the twentieth century, it was Jewish Americans. As with many black players today, basketball seemed like a way out of their poverty for immigrant Jewish players. Basketball scholarships were one

of the few ways low-income Jewish men could afford a college education. Stereotypes of the time suggested that Jewish players were inherently better at basketball because "the game places a premium on an alert,
scheming mind, flashy trickiness, artful dodging and general smart aleck-
ness."[37] These were all qualities believed to be held by Jewish people. In
addition, experts believed Jewish players were generally shorter, and that
gave them better balance and speed. That a hundred years ago the assumption was that being shorter made a person better at basketball is a
good example of how our beliefs about sport and ability change over
time, along with which group is seen as best suited to play it.

As Jewish Americans achieved social mobility, many of them moved
out of those dense, urban environments and were replaced by the suc-
ceeding waves of migrants. In many U.S. cities, this included African
Americans moving out of the South to escape the physical and economic
violence of Jim Crow segregation. Termed the Great Migration, this
movement changed the racial map of the United States as segregation
moved from being regional (with most black Americans living in the
rural South) to urban (with African American people concentrated in
inner cities). The same pattern is visible in boxing, another sport that
lends itself to city life, where a gym takes up even less space than a
basketball court. In the early twentieth century, the white boxers Jack
Johnson fought against for the world title were of Irish (John L. Sullivan)
or Italian (Tommy Burns) descent.[38] White ethnic boxers dominated until
the success of Joe Louis, when African Americans took center stage. In
the twenty-first century, boxing includes a mix of black, Latino, Eastern
European, and Filipino athletes.

THE ROONEY RULE: COACHES,
MANAGERS, AND OWNERS

Both basketball and boxing have historically provided opportunities for
different racial and ethnic groups. Are sports in general a path toward
upward mobility for groups marginalized by the wider society? In the
United States, stories about players whose entrance into professional
leagues allows them to pull their family out of poverty are a standard
trope. These stories ignore the thousands of players who never make it to
the professional level. Among the 18,000 men playing NCAA college

basketball, only 1.2 percent will ever play at the professional level. For women basketball players, the numbers are even worse at .9 percent. In women's soccer, the odds of going pro are 1,756 to 1.[39] In NCAA football, 1.6 percent will go on to play professionally, while the best odds are for baseball, with 9.8 percent of all players moving on to the next level.[40] It's important to note that the numbers for baseball are high because of its minor league system, which provides many more spots than the NFL or the NBA. Of those drafted into the baseball minor leagues, only 17.6 percent will ever make it to the majors.[41]

The odds of making it to the professional level are low, and the path becomes even more difficult when we consider a lifelong career in sports beyond the field. We've already seen how stacking contributes to the lack of coaches of color in the NFL, where there are only 8 head coaches of color out of 32 teams.[42] In the MLB, though 41 percent of the league is made up of players of color (African American, Latino, or Asian), only 5 of the general managers on 30 teams are people of color, and this is the highest percentage the league has ever achieved. In the NBA, 9 people of color are head coaches out of 30 total teams.[43] The MLB does slightly better in its front office, where 33 percent of employees are people of color. In the NFL, 26 percent of its front office employees are people of color, while the NBA does best at 36.4 percent.[44] All of these figures demonstrate that, despite their large numbers on the field, players of color do not make it into the higher ranks of the sports world in the same numbers.

In 2003 the NFL, led by the late Pittsburgh Steelers owner Dan Rooney, took proactive measures to increase its diversity at the coaching level. What came to be called the Rooney Rule initially dictated that every team with a head coaching vacancy interview at least one or more diverse candidates as part of their search. In 2009, the rule was expanded to include general manager positions and other front office positions.[45] The success of the rule is mixed. The eight minority coaches in 2017 was a record high for the league. But after the 2018 season, of the seven vacant head coaching positions, all were filled by white men, meaning that in the 2019 season, there may only be three minority head coaches. Accounts of how coaching searches have gone suggest that some teams pay only lip service to the rule. The Oakland Raiders interviewed minority candidates for their vacant head coaching position, but a *USA Today* report suggested that the owners had already reached an agreement to hire

John Gruden, who is white. The interviews, then, were purely for show.[46] Additional analyses suggest that when black coaches are hired, they aren't given tenures as long as their white counterparts, meaning they aren't given as much time to prove themselves before they're fired. This is true even when black head coaches win more frequently than their white counterparts.[47]

There is no Rooney Rule for team ownership, and the numbers become even starker when we look at the people who have the most power and control, as well as the most financial gain to be reaped. There is only one majority owner of color in the MLB—Arturo Moreno, owner of the Los Angeles Angels.[48] In the NFL, two teams—the Jacksonville Jaguars and the Buffalo Bills—are owned by people of color. Three NBA teams are majority owned by people of color: the Charlotte Hornets, Sacramento Kings, and Milwaukee Bucks. It's not surprising that there is such a stark lack of diversity among the owners of professional sports teams in the United States. Estimates suggest that white men account for 72 percent of corporate leadership at Fortune 500 companies.[49]

The racial and gender makeup of owners affects the decisions that impact the players on the field, often with racial implications. In response to the protests of many NFL players, who took a knee or refused to stand or stayed in the locker room during the national anthem in order to protest police brutality against African Americans, NFL owners were uncertain about how to handle the issues. Their responses tended to be more concerned with profits than with social justice. Houston Texans owner Robert McNair infuriated players when he said about the situation, "We can't have the inmates running the prison."[50] His comment suggested both that the players were all criminals and that, within the metaphor, owners were the prison guards. McNair apologized, but then also backstepped by saying his comment referred to owners rather than players. In addition, though the owners have the power to set rules for punishing players for behavior, the same rules don't apply to the owners themselves. Owners have been caught soliciting prostitutes, engaging in racketeering, drunk driving, sexually harassing their employees, and cheating on their taxes. Most media narratives focus on the deviance of players, who are disproportionately black or Latino, but not on the criminal behavior of owners, who are mostly white men. This dynamic mirrors society in general, where most conversations about crime focus on crimes of poverty rather than on white-collar crime. In sports, as in the larger world, the repercussions for your behaviors—whether what you do is considered a crime as well as what happens to you if you're caught—is very much influenced by your race.

JACK JOHNSON TO SERENA WILLIAMS: HOW FAR WE'VE COME AND HOW FAR WE HAVE TO GO

When Jack Johnson beat Jim Jeffries, cartoons lamented his victory as a defeat for the white race. Cartoons drawn of Johnson were consistent with existing stereotypes of African American people. His features were exaggerated, making his eyes whiter and his lips bigger. Images like these served a very specific purpose—to create and reinforce the idea of black people as something other than human beings.

Though progress has been made in the wider world as well as within sports in the last 120 years, many of these ideas are still with us. In 2018 an Australian newspaper, the *Herald Sun*, published a cartoon of Serena Williams after her loss in the U.S. Open that depicted her in a style eerily reminiscent of images from Johnson's time period. Her facial features are made unrecognizable, with large lips, while her body is blown up, making her appear ape-like. Williams is made to look inhuman, and though many observers pointed to the racist and sexist nature of the image, the Australian Press Council defended it, calling it a "non-racist caricature familiar to most Australian readers."[51] As we'll see in the next chapter, sports can certainly sometimes serve as an avenue for positive change and this has often been true as it relates to race and ethnicity. But there's still a lot of progress to be made.

9

RIDING A BIKE, RAISING A FIST, AND TAKING A KNEE

The Long History of Sports, Activism, and Social Change

"**M**any a woman is riding to suffrage on a bicycle," Elizabeth Cady Stanton said in 1895, 25 years before suffragettes (women who advocated for their right to vote) finally achieved their dream of the vote for women. Susan B. Anthony, another famous suffragette, agreed with Stanton about the use of bicycles as a tool for women's liberation, as she noted the feelings of freedom and self-reliance the new mode of transportation provided to women. Both the women fighting for women's rights and those opposed to the movement acknowledged the strong connection between the bicycle and social change. Why were bicycles so important?

Before the bicycle, the options available to middle- and upper-class women for getting around were limited. If their family owned one, they could take a carriage, but they had to be chaperoned and the carriage probably belonged to their husband or father. A woman couldn't drive the carriage herself, so there was the expense and encumbrance of servants. Middle- and upper-class women most often would have had to ask permission to take out a carriage owned by their family, and carriages for hire cost money, which they were unlikely to have. Horseback was another option, but again, the horse probably wasn't theirs, and they still had to be escorted. Also, it wasn't acceptable for middle- and upper-class women to travel too quickly on a horse.[1] For that matter, going fast wasn't feasible for women who rode sidesaddle, the preferred feminine style of riding that prevented women from straddling a horse but also made their position rather precarious. Walking was an option, but it was slow and respectable women couldn't be seen wandering around by themselves. To be seen walking in general was suspect for many nineteenth-century middle- and upper-class women, who spent most of their lives indoors or in a few acceptable public spaces. Before the bicycle, there was simply no way for many women to move around quickly and easily under their own power.

It took awhile for bicycles to become the machines that drove the feminist movement, though. At first, bicycles were called "bone-shakers" and were seen as exclusively for men. Their status as masculine accessories was based on several factors, including the fact that they couldn't be ridden sidesaddle. When the safety bicycle was invented, all that began to change. The safety bicycle had two wheels that were the same size (as opposed to a much larger front wheel) and had inflated tires. This bicycle was deemed safe for children, and some women decided it was safe for them, too. Women took to bicycles, which they called velocipedes, and the women who rode them, velocipedestriennes. The sight of women riding around on their bicycles inspired all kinds of fears, including concerns that the act of straddling a bicycle would contribute to women's sexual liberation by inducing repeated orgasms. Some critics thought the exercise of cycling would make women better equipped to become pregnant, while others worried their internal organs would be rattled, making them susceptible to everything from tuberculosis to gout. There were even concerns about what was called "bicycle face," the expression of tense concentration while riding that would render women unattractive.[2]

Bicycles were also an important incentive in the move away from restrictive clothing for women. The long skirt was on its way out by 1868, when the contestants in the world's earliest women's cycling race wore short skirts to help them pedal more effectively and avoid accidents. The problem with skirts and accidents was real, as the skirts often got wound so tightly around the pedals women found it impossible to even get up after they'd fallen to unwind them. Bicycling bloomers, or a "bicycling costume," were still long (ankle length) and quite puffy. But they provided more freedom of movement and made riding a bit safer. Some men swore not to speak to women who wore the new bloomers, while others admired the view of women's legs the new costume provided.[3]

The bicycle became deeply associated with the idea of the New Woman, who didn't want to have children and might actually want a career and a political voice of her own. Cartoons of the time depicted the New Woman on her bike, her children and husband suffering at home without her. When Cambridge, the elite British university, admitted women for the first time in 1897, male students protested by hanging a woman on a bicycle in effigy. British suffragettes would ride on their bicycles with "Votes for Women" banners in the 1910s, and they used bicycles to block Winston Churchill's motorcade as part of a demonstration for the women's vote. The suffragette movement even had its own bicycle, complete with the colors of the movement and a "Medallion of Freedom." As described by one historian, bicycles for women were "a steed on which they rode into a new world."[4]

SACRED OR PROFANE?
THE QUESTION OF SPORT AND PROTEST

Bicycles were an important part of the nineteenth- and early twentieth-century movement for women's rights. In other settings, should sports be used as a venue for social activism and change? Or do sports exist in a realm above and beyond what some people refer to as "mere" politics? A contemporary situation in which these questions have played out is the movement within the National Football League (NFL) for players to kneel during the national anthem. Mostly African American players have used their NFL platform to bring attention to the problem of police brutality, including the murders of young black men like Michael Brown, Eric Garner, and Tamir Rice, as well as black women like Charleena Lyles, Shukri Ali, and Aiyana Stanley-Jones. NFL team owners and critics outside the sport, including President Donald Trump, have repeatedly condemned protesting players, including most recently, Megan Rapinoe, a white member of the World Cup–champion U.S. women's soccer team who began kneeling during the anthem in 2016. The critics argue that sports is no place for such displays. These arguments are hardly new, having been heard over and over again when athletes use their sport to make a stand. What is it about sports that causes people to argue it should be held separate from the problems and issues that plague the rest of society?

As an institution, sport is undeniably a microcosm of society. There's no reason to expect that all the inequalities, prejudice, and bigotry that exist in the wider world will disappear when we walk onto the field or the court. But sport also has some unique qualities compared to other institutions like education or government. In fact, the institution sport resembles most closely is religion, as sport shares religion's quality of mystique and nostalgia. The fervor and emotion many fans bring to their favorite team comes close at times to cult-like proportions. Like religion, sport makes us cry, lifts us up, and sometimes, gives us a purpose. The transcendental experience we can have watching our favorite team win the championship is similar to the collective effervescence that comes from religious ritual. Like religion, sports fandom is often seen as something you're born into, and there may be repercussions if you change your team affiliation later on—namely, being accused of being a fair-weather fan.

Sports can serve a function that's similar to that of religion—sorting the world into what is sacred and what's profane. Examples of the sacred, that which is set aside and apart from everyday life, might include a certain spot on the field (the star in the middle of the Dallas Cowboys home field) or a ritual (the haka performed by New Zealand's All Black rugby team before each game). You can tell when something's been set aside as sacred by the reaction that comes when it's violated in some way. When wide receiver Terrell Owens, a player on the opposing team, celebrated on the Dallas Cowboys' star after scoring a touchdown, fans were upset, feeling that he'd violated an important norm of the game. In the case of NFL players and their protests, the arguments revealed the ways in which many people felt that standing during the national anthem was sacred.

If you believe sport is sacred, then you would feel it should exist on a plane separate from the profane world of social issues, inequality, and politics. But the reality is that no part of our social lives exists in a pure vacuum. Even if any form of protest were kept out of sport, the institution would still be political, representing the politics of the status quo. Though it's difficult for most people to see, choosing not to protest or work for change is its own kind of passive activism in support of keeping things the way they are. All of which isn't to say that there aren't constraints on athletes and others in the sports world when they use their platform for a social cause. As with social activism in any area, there are costs and constraints, as well as opportunities and rewards.

HOW HISTORY ERASED WILMA RUDOLPH

Many athletes have learned the costs associated with taking up the mantle of social activism. Some of them, like Jackie Robinson, are still celebrated for being pathbreakers. Others, like Olympic runner and civil rights activist Wilma Rudolph, are mostly forgotten. Rudolph was a contemporary of Robinson, becoming the first American woman to win three gold medals at a single Olympic Games. Rudolph grew up near Clarksville, Tennessee, one of 22 children from her father's two marriages. At four, she contracted polio and had to use a knee brace just to walk. Her siblings took turns massaging her leg every day, and her mother, Blanche, who was a domestic worker, drove her 90 miles to Nashville for therapy. When the brace came off, at age nine Rudolph had to learn to walk all over again. Yet at the age of 16, she won her first Olympic medal. Rudolph's success turned her into a global sensation overnight. Italian newspapers called her "The Black Gazelle." Rudolph was wholesome, personable, and beautiful—a ready-made media darling. She was so famous, she was known simply by her first name—Wilma.[5]

Rudolph won her three gold medals in 1960, right in the middle of the Cold War and the burgeoning civil rights movement. Her success at the Olympics made her an important symbol in the propaganda war the United States was engaged in with the Soviet bloc. Even without the state-sponsored sports programs that were standard in the Soviet Union, the United States wanted the world to believe that it was still capable of producing elite athletes. Of course, the irony was that when Rudolph came back to her hometown, it was still deeply segregated. In fact, given that the governor of her home state at the time was a self-declared "old-fashioned segregationist," Rudolph had to insist that her homecoming parade be racially integrated. Her parade and banquet became the first integrated events in the history of her hometown of Clarksville.

Because of Rudolph's fame and these Cold War politics, she was appointed a goodwill ambassador for the United States in 1963. Rudolph's job was to travel to African countries that were threatened by the spread of communism. As an African American, Rudolph was pressured to use her own example to persuade African people that the United States, despite the images of brutality against black civil rights protesters in the South, really wasn't all that bad. It was during this tour that Rudolph became especially politicized, witnessing the legacy of colonialism and political resistance movements in French West Africa. Rudolph wrote about feeling, during her tour, that she was among *her* people. When she came back to the United States, she immediately joined a protest to integrate restaurants in her hometown. With Rudolph's involvement, the Clarksville Shoney's was soon integrated, followed by the city pool and city parks. She was just 23 years old and already having an important impact on the world.[6]

Sports historians argue Rudolph was seen as apolitical by the media, and this is why her activism now gets left out of her story. In fact, as America's sweetheart, she had to be apolitical. As sociologist and civil rights activist Harry Edwards said of Rudolph, "And it [her civil rights activism] was never fully documented or recognized by the mainstream American sports media because that's not the Wilma that they wanted to project, that they wanted to exist."[7] When most people today remember Wilma Rudolph, this aspect of her life is largely ignored. Perhaps because of her activism, Rudolph fell out of the public eye at a fairly young age. That her fame was so short-lived might also have to do with the intersection of her identities as both an African American and a woman. As Rudolph herself said in a 1978 interview, "There's never been a black woman that has had a top endorsement for any athletic equipment company. So that is still there, and there's still a fight and still a struggle."[8] In her memoir, Rudolph talks about her dissatisfaction, noting that of all the places she thought she'd end up, it wasn't back in her hometown of Clarksville. Like many African American women, the consequences for Rudolph's activism were compounded by her race and her gender. And until Serena and Venus Williams in the twenty-first century, there were still no black women athletes with top endorsements.

CURT FLOOD AND THE RESERVE CLAUSE IN BASEBALL

Athletes like Wilma Rudolph used their fame to affect injustice outside their sport. Other athletes have worked to make changes on the court or the field. Billie Jean King, an American tennis player, was a pioneer in demanding equal reward and recognition for women's tennis. When it was clear the existing tournaments weren't interested in treating women equally, King led the charge for women to break out on their own, starting the Virginia Slims Tour. She was instrumental in the formation of a player's union, the Women's Tennis Association. Because of her insistence and resolve, the U.S. Open became the first tournament to pay women and men equal prize money in 1973.[9]

It's hard to imagine in the current cultural climate, in which top athletes are seen as overpaid, that in the past many professional athletes could barely make a living at their sport. Unions like the Women's Tennis Association were important for giving athletes some control and negotiating power. In sports like baseball, players had little control over their careers and no power to demand that things be different. The reserve clause in Major League Baseball stated that even after a player's contract had expired, the rights to the player were retained by the team. Players were not free to enter into a contract with another team, which meant that players were largely at the whim of the team with whom they'd signed a contract. They could be reassigned, traded, sold, or released without any say in the decision. Their careers were mostly out of their control.[10]

Curt Flood, along with Marvin Miller, changed all that. Marvin Miller had formerly worked for the United Steelworkers union before becoming head of the player's union in 1966. At the time, MLB players had a fake union, the Players Association, that had been formed by the owners. The Players Association started in order to fend off player attempts to unionize as well as to keep players from leaving to go play for a league that had been formed in Mexico and offered better pay. When Miller took over, it was still difficult to convince many players of the benefits of unionizing. The league had convinced players they should feel lucky to be playing, rather than raising concerns about their declining pensions or their share of the growing income from television rights.[11]

At the same time, in the world outside of baseball, social movements were everywhere, including the civil rights movement. The framework provided by the civil rights movement and the Black Power movement made it easier for many African American players to understand the need for a union. Curt Flood was one of those players. Born in Oakland, California, Flood played for the St. Louis Cardinals. Flood was shocked and outraged by the system of segregation he faced playing on Southern minor league teams, where he couldn't stay in the same hotels as his white teammates and had to eat in the kitchen at segregated restaurants. In October 1969, Flood was traded to the Phillies without being either consulted or informed. He heard about the decision on the radio rather than from ownership. He decided the time had come to challenge the reserve clause.[12]

Flood consulted Miller and traveled to the union's executive board meeting in December, where he secured his fellow players' unanimous support. Flood was taking a big risk with his career and financial future in the face of odds that Miller and his fellow players knew were stacked against him. As Miller recalled, "[Flood] thought about that [the odds] a little while and he said, 'But if we won the case, wouldn't that benefit all the other players?' And I said, oh yes. 'And all the players to come?' And I said, oh yes, and he said, 'that's good enough for me.'"[13] The All-Star, with a promising career still ahead of him, wrote a letter to the commissioner, in which he famously stated, "After 12 years in the major leagues I do not feel that I am a piece of property to be bought and sold irrespective of my wishes."[14]

Because he refused to sign a contract with the Phillies, Flood was shut out of the 1970 baseball season. His case against the reserve clause went all the way to the Supreme Court, where the justices ruled against him and his fellow players in a 5–3 decision. But the players had come together in their support for Flood, and the tide had turned. Miller no longer had to convince players that they deserved free agency—the right to have some say about where, when, and how they played. In 1972, the players went on strike and were able to convince the owners to accept binding arbitration for contract disputes, a process in which a person independent from the owners helps make decisions about a fair salary for players. In 1975, two players (Dave McNally and Andy Messersmith) refused to sign their contracts and played a year without a contract. The following year they contended they were "free agents." Independent arbitration ruled in favor of McNally and Nessersmith and, though the league challenged the ruling, the decision was upheld. Eighty years of the reserve system ended, but Curt Flood paid the price. Though he played in the 1971 season, he quit after 18 games due to mistreatment by the league and anti-union teammates. He never played major league baseball again.

With the advent of free agency, the salaries of players, as well as their control over their careers, improved. In 2019, Bryce Harper, the top free agent, signed a record-setting deal for $330 million over 13 years. More importantly, the percentage of the total profits from the league that goes to players in the MLB hovers at around 50 percent, though it fell below that in the 2018 season. Complaints about the salaries of professional athletes need to be balanced against this backdrop. As astronomical as the salaries of players like Bryce Harper appear, they pale in comparison to the profits made by owners. In 2017, Major League Baseball as an organization made over $10 billion in revenue.[15] The richest MLB owner, Charles Johnson, has a net worth of $6.4 billion (the 20th richest MLB owner is worth a mere $700 million).[16] To buy a team costs between $800 million (for the San Diego Padres) to $2.15 billion (for the Los Angeles Dodgers).[17] There's certainly a great deal of money to be made from professional sports, but in none of the big three leagues in the United States does the share of profits going to players exceed about 50 percent. In the NFL the salary cap system keeps the number at 48.5 percent while in the NBA, it's set at 50 percent.[18] That's half the profits divided between 30 owners for the MLB and NBA and 32 owners for the NFL, compared to 1200, 1696, and 494 players, respectively.

THE POWERLESSNESS OF COLLEGE ATHLETES

Inequalities exist between the profits owners reap from their teams and the salaries their players make, but professional athletes do at least get paid. At the elite level of collegiate sports, players make millions of dollars for their programs with no compensation beyond their athletic scholarships. In some instances, those scholarships don't cover the full costs of attending college, but prohibit athletes from earning any extra money beyond their scholarship. The same rules don't apply to students receiving academic scholarships. While academic scholarships often provide for school supplies, transportation, and entertainment, athletic scholarships do not. This inequality between the two different types of scholarships exists against the backdrop of the millions of dollars made by universities from their sports programs. In basketball, the NCAA makes $1 billion annually from its television broadcasting contract for March Madness alone. The president of the NCAA earns $1.7 million, while the 10 highest paid college coaches in March Madness make between $2 and $9 million.[19]

College players have no union or association to protect their rights and, unlike professional athletes, they lack financial resources as well. Protest and social activism at this level carries with it even more risks, but players do sometimes raise their voices. In 1970, nine African American football players were inspired by the legacy of Jim Brown and other player-activists to boycott the team. They became known in the media as the Syracuse 8, even though the boycott actually involved nine players. They were protesting the subtle and sometimes not-so-subtle racism they encountered on the university campus. For example, running back Greg Allen was told by his coach moments after setting foot in Syracuse that he was not allowed to date white women. Players who wanted to major in engineering or biology were told they couldn't because the classes would be too hard, though the same policy did not apply to white players.

The nine players drafted a petition with a set of demands, some of which benefitted black players and some addressing larger team issues. They asked that black and white players be given the same access to academic advisors and tutors, to correct for the inequalities in what classes they were allowed to take. They also sought to correct inequalities in playing time. As a racially integrated team, Syracuse couldn't play any of the schools south of the "Cotton Curtain," schools that weren't racially integrated and refused to play any teams that were. But many northern schools still followed unofficial rules about black and white playing time. As Dana Harrell, one of the boycotting players, described, "You could have three outstanding [African American] halfbacks, but you wouldn't play them all together, because you didn't want the 'big money boosters'— that's what I call them—the big money boosters to accuse the program of going black." Similar informal quota systems existed across sports in the United States at the time. Teams were technically integrated, but coaches, managers, and owners made sure that the percentage of black players never exceeded a certain level. The Syracuse players believed that having a black assistant coach would solve many of these problems, but their head coach had no intention of listening to their demands. He called Greg Allen into his office and told him he had to choose between being a football player and being black. When no actions had been taken by spring, the players decided to boycott the spring practice.[20]

Their intentions didn't extend beyond a boycott of that one practice. They didn't want to put the program at risk, so they weren't going to sit out of a game or an alumni event. But when the media learned of the players' actions, they became labeled "black militants" or "black dissidents" or simply, "the blacks." The players were suspended from the team and some of their white teammates threatened to boycott the team if the black players were allowed to return. Alumni wrote to the university demanding that the players be kicked off the team and that their scholarships be revoked. The players went home for the summer, with no idea what the eventual outcome would be. When they returned in the fall, a black assistant coach had been hired, but he was a coach in name only. The black coach slept during team meetings and was completely ignored by the rest of the white staff. The players decided to boycott the season.[21]

Despite widespread hostility, the chancellor of the university, along with a group of faculty, demanded that the players keep their scholarships. All nine of them graduated from Syracuse, four going on to earn master's degrees. Dana Harrell went to law school. They started seeing changes at Syracuse, even if they had to watch the football team from the sidelines. But Greg Allen, who had been contacted by NFL scouts before the boycott, ended up playing in the Canadian Football League after he graduated instead of playing in the United States. Even there, his coach eventually let him go, not for his lack of athletic ability but because of his "baggage." In 2006, the nine players were invited back to Syracuse where they received a formal apology and the Chancellor's Medal, the university's highest honor.[22]

Following in the footsteps of the Syracuse 8, in 2015 the University of Missouri football team lent their weight to protests about the racial climate on their campus. When a student organization began calling for the resignation of the president, who had proved unresponsive to the concerns of African American students, the football team joined in. The players wrote a letter stating that they would not participate in any football-related activities until the president resigned. The initial letter came from the players of color, but the coach backed them up, stating that the whole team was united behind their cause. Within days, the president had resigned.[23]

REPUBLICANS BUY SNEAKERS, TOO

Thirty years before Colin Kaepernick started kneeling, Mahmoud Abdul-Rauf was suspended by the NBA and fined $32,000 for refusing to participate in the national anthem pre-game ceremony. The league and Abdul-Rauf eventually reached an agreement allowing him to stand and pray during the national anthem, but Abdul-Rauf was still punished for his politics. He was traded away from the Denver Nuggets. The former All-Star and contestant in the slam-dunk contest found himself playing fewer and fewer minutes. He lost his starting spot and, when his contract expired in 1998, he couldn't even get a tryout with another NBA team despite being only 29 years old.[24] Craig Hodges's career in the NBA also ended over his controversial stand against racism, including suggesting that players Michael Jordan and Michael Johnson walk out during the NBA finals as a stand in solidarity with the black community.[25] When Tommie Smith and John Carlos, Olympic medalists in 1968, famously raised their fists in the Black Power salute on the podium, they were kicked out of the Olympic village and referred to on the air as "black-skinned stormtroopers."[26]

The list of athletes who have paid the price for their activism in one way or another is long, with new names still being added. Perhaps that long legacy explains a famous quote from NBA star Michael Jordan. In the 1990s, Jordan had achieved worldwide fame. The logo for his Air Jordan shoes was among one of the most recognizable symbols on the planet. Jordan was famously apolitical and was asked why he wouldn't support a candidate running against right-wing U.S. Senator Jesse Helms in his home state of North Carolina. "Republicans buy sneakers, too," was Jordan's famous response. His fellow NBA star, Charles Barkley, took a different tack, declaring, "I don't have to be what you want me to be," and speaking out unapologetically on social issues of the day. But even as Barkley continues to encourage the next generation of athlete-activists to speak out, he acknowledges that his approach probably lost him $10 million in endorsements over the course of his career, as well as subjecting him to criticism from the front office of his team, the league, and the media.[27]

On the other side of the spectrum, athletes who support socially conservative agendas often go unremarked and unpunished. In 2017, first basemen Yuli Gurriel was caught on camera making a racist gesture directed at pitcher Yu Darvish, a player of Japanese and Iranian descent. Gurriel pulled his eyelids into a slant and mouthed a racial epithet. Gurriel was punished with what many critics saw as a slap on the wrist, a five-game suspension for the next season, rather than one that took effect during the World Series. Not surprisingly, fans started imitating Gurriel's gesture and posting photos on social media.[28] In 2019, the San Francisco 49ers drafted Nick Bosa as their second overall pick in the draft. Bosa is a supporter of Donald Trump who had to scrub his social media accounts before the draft because of his affection for white nationalist Twitter accounts. The 49ers are the same team for which Colin Kaepernick played, making it especially ironic that Bosa's politics were largely ignored. One expert on the draft revealed the double standard at play when he said about Bosa's prospects, "I don't think it's going to affect his draft stock. I can't imagine—and I've talked to some teams—a team saying we're gonna pass on this guy because he's left or right wing."[29]

THE FUTURE OF SPORTS ACTIVISM

All sports reflect some set of values and beliefs. The question is whether those values and beliefs are made explicit or remain hidden. When women's sports are given less media coverage, less promotion, and the women playing them receive fewer rewards, sport reflects the belief that women's activities are not as important as men's. In other words, sport reinforces gender inequality. When sports commentators emphasize the appearance of African American women over their athletic ability, they're reflecting a set of values and beliefs. When NFL owners and critics attack players who protest police brutality, they do so out of a mind-set that denies the real racial inequality that still exists in the United States. Sport will always reflect a certain set of values and beliefs, so the question is, which values and beliefs?

In the past, players have often paid a high price for challenging the existing values and beliefs in their sport. Athlete-activists have lost money, endorsements, and, often, the ability to go on playing the game they love. But perhaps the tide is turning. Recent social movements like Black Lives Matter and #MeToo have perhaps had an effect on sports culture, making it easier for some athletes to include activism as part of their brand. Players are encouraged to stand for something and use their platform to challenge the status quo. Soccer star Ali Krieger, another member of the USWNT who is also engaged to fellow player Ashlyn Harris, said, "I also understand that I have a platform to really help change the way people think about soccer [football]." The idea that fame comes with a level of responsibility is normal, at least for Krieger.[30]

Though Colin Kaepernick's protest ultimately resulted in the end of his NFL career, his actions had ripple effects across the sporting world. In the WNBA, Minnesota Lynx players spoke up about victims of police violence like Philando Castile. During the 2017 final, members of the Los Angeles Sparks stayed in their locker room during the national anthem. Some players wanted to kneel while others didn't, so in the interest of team unity, the whole team stayed in the locker room. Player protests spread to the MLB and the NHL, while in the NFL, white players like Chris Long and Seth DeValve showed their solidarity with their black teammates by taking their own knee, or in the case of Chris Long, donating his entire year's salary to charities. At the college level, Gyree Durante, backup quarterback at Albright College, took a knee before a game in October 2017 and was then cut from the team. In high school, Darius Moore's protest during the national anthem made him the target for racial epithets. Even cheerleaders have gotten involved, with squads at both Kennesaw State and Howard University taking a knee during the playing of the national anthem.[31] Perhaps all these examples are evidence of a new era of sports activism.

As we've explored throughout this book, social change happens in sport, whether intentional or not. Cheerleading goes from being seen as the manliest of activities to mostly for girls. The rules about who gets to play and who doesn't change over time. Our sense of whether women can or should be athletes evolves. Globalization spreads some sports from one part of the world to another. Change in sport, as in the rest of the world, is a constant. The question that remains is: Will those changes be in the direction of a playing field that's more accessible and equal for everyone?

NOTES

I. WHEN ALL CHEERLEADERS WERE BOYS

1. Jaime Schultz, *Qualifying Times: Points of Change in U.S. Women's Sports* (Urbana: University of Illinois Press, 2014), 170.
2. Elizabeth Sherman, "Why Don't More People Consider Cheerleading a Sport?" *The Atlantic*, May 2, 2017, https://www.theatlantic.com/entertainment/archive/2017/05/why-dont-more-people-consider-competitive-cheerleading-a-sport/524940/ (accessed February 5, 2019).
3. Schultz, *Qualifying Times*, 170.
4. Ibid., 171.
5. Ibid., 173.
6. Ibid.
7. Ibid., 75.
8. Ibid., 174–76.
9. Sally Jenkins, "History of Women's Basketball," WNBA, July 3, 1997, https://www.wnba.com/news/history-of-womens-basketball/ (accessed February 5, 2019).
10. Schultz, *Qualifying Times*, 76.
11. Ibid., 79.
12. Ibid., 81–82.
13. Ibid., 84.
14. Ibid., 173.
15. Ibid., 173–74.
16. Ibid., 84–85.
17. "LPGA Teaching and Club Professionals: A History," LGPA, n.d., http://www.lpga.com/tcp/historytcp (accessed February 5, 2019).

18. Bill Francis, "League of Women Ballplayers," National Baseball Hall of Fame, n.d., https://baseballhall.org/discover-more/stories/baseball-history/league-of-women-ballplayers (accessed February 5, 2019).

19. "A History of Women in Formula One," CNN Sports, August 21, 2018, https://www.cnn.com/2018/08/21/motorsport/gallery/women-in-formula-one-spt-intl/index.html (accessed February 5, 2019).

20. "Danica Patrick and the Women of NASCAR," ABCNews, n.d., https://abcnews.go.com/Business/photos/women-nascar-danica-patrick-indy-500-14343965/image-19000228 (accessed February 5, 2019).

21. Sherry Mabron Gordon, *Women Athletes* (Berkeley Heights, NJ: Enslow Publishing, 2017), 48; Ed Zieralski, "Timeline: Horse Racing's Women Jockeys," *San Diego Union-Tribune*, June 8, 2013, https://www.sandiegouniontribune.com/sports/horse-racing/sdut-women-jockeys-horse-racing-2013jun08-htmlstory.html (accessed February 5, 2019).

22. Karen Blumenthal, *Let Me Play: The Story of Title IX, the Law That Changed the Future of Girls in America* (New York: Athaneum Books, 2005), 41–44.

23. "Woman Kicks Extra Points," *New York Times*, October 20, 1997, https://www.nytimes.com/1997/10/20/sports/woman-kicks-extra-points.html (accessed February 13, 2019).

24. Jake Simpson, "How Title IX Sneakily Revolutionized Women's Sports," *The Atlantic*, June 21, 2012, https://www.theatlantic.com/entertainment/archive/2012/06/how-title-ix-sneakily-revolutionized-womens-sports/258708/ (accessed February 13, 2019).

25. Blumenthal, *Let Me Play*, 38; Kristina Chan, "The Mother of Title IX: Patsy Mink," *The She Network*, April 24, 2012, https://www.womenssportsfoundation.org/education/mother-title-ix-patsy-mink/ (accessed February 13, 2019).

26. Simpson, "How Title IX Sneakily Revolutionized Women's Sports."

27. Barbara Winslow, "The Impact of Title IX," *History Now: The Journal of the Gilder Lehrman Institute of American History*, September 24, 2016, https://faculty.uml.edu/sgallagher/The_Impact_of_Title_IX-_GilderLehrman.pdf (accessed February 13, 2019); Jeaah Lee and Maya Dusenbery, "Charts: The State of Women's Athletics, 40 Years after Title IX," *Mother Jones*, June 22, 2012, https://www.motherjones.com/politics/2012/06/charts-womens-athletics-title-nine-ncaa/ (accessed February 13, 2019).

28. Winslow, "The Impact of Title IX."

29. Lee and Dusenbery, "Charts."

30. Alana Semuels, "Poor Girls Are Leaving Their Brothers Behind," *The Atlantic*, November 27, 2017, https://www.theatlantic.com/business/archive/2017/11/gender-education-gap/546677/ (accessed February 13, 2019).

31. Schultz, *Qualifying Times*, 131–33; Blumenthal, *Let Me Play*, 65–74.

32. Blumenthal, *Let Me Play*, 41–46.

33. Dominque Debucquoy-Dodley, "NJ Youth Basketball Team Forfeits, Won't Play Season without Girl Teammates," CNN, February 16, 2017, https://www.cnn.com/2017/02/13/us/kid-basketball-season-trnd/index.html (accessed February 13, 2019).

34. Debucquoy-Dodley, "NJ Youth Basketball Team Forfeits."

35. Eric Anderson, "'I Used to Think Women Were Weak': Orthodox Masculinity, Gender Segregation, and Sport," *Sociological Forum* 23, no. 2 (2008): 260.

36. Anderson, "'I Used to Think Women Were Weak,'" 271.

2. HOW TO TELL IF A WOMAN IS "REALLY" A WOMAN

1. Jaime Schultz, *Qualifying Times: Points of Change in U.S. Women's Sports* (Urbana: University of Illinois Press, 2014), 118.

2. Ibid., 118.

3. Ruth Padawer, "The Humiliating Practice of Sex-Testing Female Athletes," *New York Times Magazine*, June 28, 2016, https://www.nytimes.com/2016/07/03/magazine/the-humiliating-practice-of-sex-testing-female-athletes.html (accessed July 16, 2019).

4. Schultz, *Qualifying Times*, 104.

5. Ibid.

6. Ibid., 104–5.

7. Ibid., 106–7.

8. Ibid., 108.

9. Ibid., 109.

10. Ibid., 110.

11. Ibid., 111–16.

12. Ibid., 117.

13. Ibid., 110.

14. "Klinefelter Syndrome," Intersex Society of North America, n.d., http://www.isna.org/faq/conditions/klinefelter (accessed February 8, 2019); "Turner Syndrome," Intersex Society of North America, n.d., http://www.isna.org/faq/conditions/turner (accessed February 8, 2019).

15. Schultz, *Qualifying Times*, 112.

16. Ibid., 117.

17. "Androgen Insensitivity Syndrome (AIS)," Intersex Society of North America, n.d., http://www.isna.org/faq/conditions/ais (accessed February 8, 2019).

18. Jamie Strashin, "What's the Real Problem with Caster Semenya?" CBC, May 14, 2018, https://www.cbc.ca/sports/olympics/trackandfield/caster-semenya-cultural-bias-1.4661929 (accessed July 5, 2019).

19. Quoted in Strashin, "What's the Real Problem with Caster Semenya?"

20. Padawer, "The Humiliating Practice."

21. Ibid.

22. Katrina Karkazis, "The Testosterone Myth," *Wired*, March 27, 2018, https://www.wired.com/story/testosterone-treatment-myth/ (accessed February 14, 2019).

23. Lisa Wade, "The New Science of Sex Difference," *Sociology Compass* 7, no. 4 (2013): 282.

24. Anne Fausto-Sterling, "Gender & Sexuality," Fields of Inquiry, n.d., http://www.annefaustosterling.com/fields-of-inquiry/gender/ (accessed February 14, 2019).

25. Katrina Karkazis, Rebecca Jordan-Young, Georgiann Davis, and Silvia Camporesi, "Out of Bounds? A Critique of the New Policies on Hyperandrogenism in Elite Female Athletes," *American Journal of Bioethics* 12, no. 7 (2012): 9.

26. Shalender Bhasin et al., "The Effects of Supraphysiologic Doses of Testosterone on Muscle Size and Strength in Normal Men," *New England Journal of Medicine* 335, no. 1 (1996): 1–7; Bent R. Ronnestad, Havard Nyaard, and Truls Raastad, "Physiological Elevation of Endogenous Hormones Result in Superior Strength and Training Adaptation," *European Journal of Applied Physiology and Occupational Physiology* 111, no. 9 (2011): 2249–59; Thomas W. Storer et al., "Testosterone Dose-Dependently Increases Maximal Voluntary Strength and Leg Power, but Does Not Affect Fatigability of Specific Tension," *Journal of Clinical Endocrinology and Metabolism* 88, no. 4 (2003): 1478–85.

27. Gail Vines, "Last Olympics for the Sex Test?" NewScientist, July 4, 1992, https://www.newscientist.com/article/mg13518284-900-last-olympics-for-the-sex-test/ (accessed February 17, 2019).

28. Karkazis et al., "Out of Bounds?" 9.

29. Kevin D. McCaul, Brian A. Gladue, and Margaret Joppa, "Winning, Losing, Mood, and Testosterone," *Hormone and Behavior* 26, no. 4 (1992): 486–504; Tania Ferreira de Oliveria, Maria Gouveia, and Rui F. Oliveria, "Testosterone Responsiveness to Winning and Losing Experiences in Female Soccer Players," *Psychoneuroendocrinology* 34, no. 7 (2009): 1056–64.

30. Schultz, *Qualifying Times*, 107.

31. Padawer, "The Humiliating Practice."

32. Nir Eynon et al., "Physiological Variables and Mitochondrial-Related Genotypes of an Athlete Who Excels in Both Short And Long-Distance Running," *Mitochondrian* 11, no. 5 (2011): 774–77; Nir Eynon et al., "The Champions' Mitochondria: Is It Genetically Determined? A review on mitochondrial DNA and elite athletic performance," *Physiological Genomics* 43, no. 13 (2011), 789–98.

33. Anna Katherine Clemmons, "7 Feet 7 and 360 Pounds with Bigger Feet Than Shaq's," *New York Times*, January 9, 2008, https://www.nytimes.com/2008/01/09/sports/ncaabasketball/09asheville.html (accessed February 17, 2019); Chris Mannix, "High Hopes: He's Three Inches Taller Than Yao Ming, but Is Pro Hoops' Biggest Player Ready for the NBA?" *Sports Illustrated*, February 12, 2007, https://www.si.com/vault/2007/02/12/8400340/high-hopes (accessed February 17, 2019).

34. Daniel M. Laby et al., "The Visual Function of Professional Baseball Players," *American Journal of Opthalmology* 122, no. 4 (1996): 476–85.

35. Jessica Ryen Doyle, "Michael Phelps Unintentionally Raises Marfan Syndrome Awareness," Foxnews.com, August 21, 2008, https://www.foxnews.com/story/michael-phelps-unintentionally-raises-marfan-syndrome-awareness (accessed February 17, 2019).

36. Susan Ninan, "Dutee Chand: I Have Found Life and Can Run without Fear Now," ESPN, April 28, 2018, http://www.espn.com/athletics/story/_/id/23336583/dutee-chand-found-life-run-fear-now (accessed February 18, 2019).

37. Sean Ingle, "Caster Semenya Accuses IAAF of Using Her as a 'Guinea Pig Experiment,'" *Guardian*, June 18, 2019, https://www.theguardian.com/sport/2019/jun/18/caster-semenya-iaaf-athletics-guinea-pig (accessed July 5, 2019).

38. Ibid.

39. Eric Niiler, "Testosterone Ruling for Athletes Fuels Debate over 'Natural' Ability," Wired, May 1, 2018, https://www.wired.com/story/testosterone-ruling-for-athletes-fuels-debate-over-natural-ability/ (accessed February 18, 2019).

3. THROWING LIKE A GIRL

1. Ruth M. Sparhawk, Mary E. Leslie, Phyllis Y. Turbow, and Zina R. Rose, *American Women in Sport, 1887–1987: A 100-Year Chronology* (Metuchen, NJ: Scarecrow, 1989), 14.

2. Iris Marion Young, *Throwing Like a Girl and Other Essays in Feminist Philosophy and Social Theory* (Bloomington: Indiana University Press, 1990), 146.

3. Karin A. Martin, "Becoming a Gendered Body: Practices of Preschools," *American Sociological Review* 63, no. 4 (1998): 498–99.

4. Ibid., 505–6.

5. Bruce Kelley and Carl Carchia, "'Hey, Data Data—Swing!" ESPN, July 11, 2013, http://www.espn.com/espn/story/_/id/9469252/hidden-demographics-youth-sports-espn-magazine (accessed March 4, 2019).

6. "Childrens' Engagement with the Outdoors and Sports Activities, UK, 2014–2015," Office for National Statistics (UK), January 30, 2018, https://www.ons.gov.uk/peoplepopulationandcommunity/wellbeing/articles/childrensengagementwiththeoutdoorsandsportsactivitiesuk/2014to2015 (accessed March 4, 2019).

7. R. Bailey, I. Wellard, and H. Dismore, "Girls' Participation in Physical Activities and Sports: Benefits, Patterns, Influences, and Ways Forward," World Health Organization, n.d., https://www.icsspe.org/sites/default/files/Girls.pdf (accessed March 4, 2019).

8. Don Sabo and Philip Veliz, "Surveying Youth Sports in America: What We Do Know and What It Means for Public Policy," in *Child's Play: Sport in Kids' Worlds*, ed. Michael Messner and Michael Musto (Rutgers, NJ: Rutgers University Press, 2016), 25.

9. Income and race also play important roles in girls' continuing participation in sports. White girls and boys in families with incomes above $65,000 show equal levels of participation, while girls of color in all income brackets have lower levels of sports participation than their boy counterparts. See Sabo and Veliz, 26.

10. "Getting More Girls in the Game of Soccer," Adidas.com, June 2019, https://www.adidas.com/us/blog/377303 (accessed July 6, 2019).

11. "Do You Know the Factors Influencing Girls' Participation in Sports?" Women's Sports Foundation, September 9, 2016, https://www.womenssportsfoundation.org/support-us/do-you-know-the-factors-influencing-girls-participation-in-sports/ (accessed March 5, 2019).

12. Attn: Twitter post, June 21, 2019, 7:00 p.m., https://twitter.com/attn/status/1142205555374608384 (accessed July 6, 2019).

13. Women's Sports Foundation, "Do You Know the Factors?"

14. Ashley Marcin, "The Average Heights of Men around the World," n.d., Healthline, https://www.healthline.com/health/average-height-for-men (accessed February 21, 2019); Vincent Iannelli, "What Is the Average Height for an Adult Woman?" VeryWellFit, October 25, 2018, https://www.verywellfit.com/average-height-for-a-woman-statistics-2632136 (accessed February 21, 2019).

15. "Tallest Man Living," Guinness World Records, n.d., http://www.guinnessworldrecords.com/world-records/tallest-man-living (accessed February 22, 2019); "Top 10 Tallest Women in the World Right Now," JustRichest, n.d., https://justrichest.com/tallest-women-world/ (accessed February 22, 2019).

16. Valerie Thibault et al., "Women and Men in Sport Performance: The Gap Has Not Evolved Since 1983," *Journal of Sports Science and Medicine* 9, no. 2 (2010): 217.

17. Laura Capranica et al., "The Gender Gap in Sports Performance: Equity Influences Equality," *International Journal of Sports Physiology and Performance* 8 (2013): 99–100.

18. Ibid., 101.

19. Melissa Matthews, "Women Are Better Athletes Than Men, Study about Gender Fitness Says," *Newsweek*, December 16, 2017, https://www.newsweek.com/women-are-better-athletes-men-study-about-gender-fitness-says-736047 (accessed March 6, 2019).

20. Alice Sanders, "Is Gender Segregation in Sports Necessary?" *How We Got to Now* (blog), July 29, 2016, http://www.pbs.org/how-we-got-to-now/blogs/howwegottonext/is-gender-segregation-in-sports-necessary/ (accessed March 6, 2019).

21. Melissa Dahl, "The Obscure Ultra-Endurance Sport Women Are Quietly Dominating," The Cut, September 11, 2016, https://www.thecut.com/2016/09/the-obscure-endurance-sport-women-are-quietly-dominating.html (accessed March 3, 2019).

22. Ibid.

23. Nadav Goldschmied and Jason Kowalczyck, "Gender Performance in the NCAA Rifle Championships: Where Is the Gap?" *Sex Roles* 74 (2014): 310.

24. Bob Cook, "Why Girls Are the Best Hope to Save Wrestling," *Forbes*, February 17, 2012, https://www.forbes.com/sites/bobcook/2012/02/17/why-girls-are-the-best-hope-to-save-wrestling/#3b115f336ae9 (accessed March 3, 2019).

25. Gary Abbott, "High School Girls Wrestling Continues Rapid Growth," National Wrestling Hall of Fame, n.d., https://nwhof.org/blog/high-school-girls-wrestling-continues-rapid-growth/ (accessed March 3, 2019).

26. Capranica et al., "Gender Gap in Sports Performance," 101.

27. Julie Kliegman, "Nothing and Everything Has Changed for the USWNT," The Ringer, June 10, 2019, https://www.theringer.com/soccer/2019/6/10/18656696/us-womens-national-team-world-cup-lawsuit-1999-megan-rapinoe (accessed July 6, 2019).

28. Leigh C. Anderson, "U.S. Men's Soccer Fails to Qualify for World Cup, Still Paid More Than Our Champion Women's Team," *Salon*, October 11, 2017, https://www.salon.com/2017/10/11/usmnt-world-cup-uswnt/ (accessed March 7, 2019); Christina Cauterucci, "The U.S. Women's Soccer Team Finally Has a Better Contract, But Not Equal Pay," *Slate*, April 5, 2017, https://slate.com/human-interest/2017/04/the-u-s-womens-soccer-team-finally-has-a-better-contract-but-not-equal-pay.html (accessed March 7, 2019).

29. David Berri, "Basketball's Growing Gender Wage Gap: The Evidence the WNBA Is Underpaying Players," *Forbes*, September 20, 2017, https://www. forbes.com/sites/davidberri/2017/09/20/there-is-a-growing-gender-wage-gap-in-professional-basketball/#4fb7664d36e0 (accessed March 7, 2019).

30. Max Saffer, "Dollars but No Sense: Golf's Long History of Shortchanging Women," ESPNW, April 8, 2016, http://www.espn.com/espnw/sports/article/15160220/big-gap-earnings-men-women-professional-golfers (accessed March 7, 2019).

31. Anderson, "U.S. Men's Soccer Fails to Qualify for World Cup."

32. Joshua Barajas, "Equal Pay for Equal Play: What the Sport of Tennis Got Right," PBS NewsHour, April 12, 2016, https://www.pbs.org/newshour/economy/equal-pay-for-equal-play-what-the-sport-of-tennis-got-right (accessed March 7, 2019).

33. "Mission and History," Women's Football Alliance, n.d., http://www.wfaprofootball.com/about/ (accessed March 8, 2019).

34. Ian Chaffee, "Forget about Sexism: Now TV Coverage of Women's Sports Is Just Plain Boring," USCNews, September 12, 2017, https://news.usc.edu/127695/forget-about-sexism-now-tv-coverage-of-womens-sports-is-just-plain-boring/ (accessed March 8, 2019).

35. Sanders, "Is Gender Segregation in Sports Necessary?"

36. Cassidy Lent, "No Minor Achievement," National Baseball Hall of Fame, n.d., https://baseballhall.org/discover/short-stops/ila-borders (accessed March 8, 2019).

37. "Yoshida Has RBI Single in First At-Bat," ESPN, May 30, 2010, http://www.espn.com/minorlbb/news/story?id=5233233 (accessed March 8, 2019).

38. Diana Pearl, "Meet the First Woman to Earn an NCAA Football Scholarship," *People*, April 14, 2017, https://people.com/sports/meet-the-first-woman-to-earn-an-ncaa-football-scholarship/ (accessed March 8, 2019).

4. SPORT FOR EVERYONE?

1. Jon Shadel, "This Gender Neutral Athlete Wants to End Sex Segregation in Sports," VICE, November 10, 2016, https://www.vice.com/en_us/article/mvk33x/this-gender-neutral-athlete-wants-to-end-sex-segregation-in-sports (accessed March 12, 2019).

2. Ibid.

3. Jaime Schultz, *Qualifying Times: Points of Change in U.S. Women's Sport* (Urbana: University of Illinois Press, 2014), 114.

4. Simon Briggs, "Why Tennis's Renée Richards, the First Transgender Woman to Play Professional Sport, Matters Today," *Telegraph*, March 30, 2018,

https://www.telegraph.co.uk/tennis/2018/03/30/tennissrenee-richards-first-transgender-woman-play-professional/ (accessed March 13, 2019).

5. Ibid.

6. Schultz, *Qualifying Times*, 114.

7. Briggs, "Why Tennis's Renée Richards."

8. Navratilova was also part of the doubles team that knocked Renée Richards out of the U.S. Open tournament in 1977; Richards later became Navratilova's coach for two years. See Briggs, "Why Tennis's Renee Richards."

9. Quoted in "Trans Athletes Make Great Gains, Yet Resentment Still Flares," NBCNews, February 25, 2019, https://www.nbcnews.com/feature/nbc-out/trans-athletes-make-great-gains-yet-resentment-still-flares-n975646 (accessed March 14, 2019).

10. "IOC Rules Transgender Athletes Can Take Part in Olympics without Surgery," *Guardian*, January 24, 2016, https://www.theguardian.com/sport/2016/jan/25/ioc-rules-transgender-athletes-can-take-part-in-olympics-without-surgery (accessed March 14, 2019).

11. Georgina Gustin, "The Olympic Committee Says Trans Athletes Can Compete without Reassignment Surgery," Medium, January 2, 2016, https://timeline.com/the-international-olympic-committee-has-nixed-the-requirement-that-transgender-athletes-have-e59a82b9e67c (accessed March 14, 2019).

12. "IOC Rules Transgender Athletes Can Take Part."

13. NCAA Office of Inclusion, *NCAA Inclusion of Transgender Athletes* (NCAA, 2011), http://www.ncaa.org/sites/default/files/Transgender_Handbook_2011_Final.pdf (accessed March 14, 2019).

14. Katherine Kornei, "This Scientist Is Racing to Discover How Gender Transitions Alter Athletic Performance—Including Her Own," *Science*, June 25, 2018, https://www.sciencemag.org/news/2018/07/scientist-racing-discover-how-gender-transitions-alter-athletic-performance-including (accessed July 15, 2019).

15. Mirin Fader, "Andraya Yearwood Knows She Has the Right to Compete," Bleacher Report, December 17, 2018, https://bleacherreport.com/articles/2810857-andraya-yearwood-knows-she-has-the-right-to-compete (accessed March 20, 2019).

16. Serena Sonoma, "Black Trans Women Want the Media to Show Them Living, Not Just Dying," *Vox*, June 18, 2019, https://www.vox.com/first-person/2019/6/18/18679295/black-trans-women-murder-violence (accessed July 6, 2019).

17. Fader, "Andraya Yearwood Knows."

18. "K–12 Policies," Transathlete, n.d., https://www.transathlete.com/k-12 (accessed March 15, 2019).

19. Gabe Murchison, *Supporting and Caring for Transgender Children*, Human Rights Campaign, September 2016, https://assets2.hrc.org/files/documents/

SupportingCaringforTransChildren.pdf?_ga=2.132362249.647985918.
1552655593-1879478770.1552655593 (accessed March 15, 2019).

20. Cyd Zeigler, *Fair Play: How LGBT Athletes Are Claiming Their Rightful Place in Sports* (Brooklyn, NY: Akashic Books, 2016), 193.

21. Pat Griffin, "Developing Policies for Transgender Students on High School Teams," National Federation of State High School Associations, September 28, 2015, http://www.nfhs.org/articles/developing-policies-for-transgender-students-on-high-school-teams/ (accessed March 15, 2019).

22. Zeigler, *Fair Play*, 193.

23. Griffin, "Developing Policies for Transgender Students."

24. Ibid.

25. George B. Cunningham and Erin E. Buzuvis, "Better Locker Rooms: It's Not Just a Transgender Thing," The Conversation, March 26, 2017, http://theconversation.com/better-locker-rooms-its-not-just-a-transgender-thing-74023 (accessed March 18, 2019).

26. Kristen Schilt and Laurel Westbrook, "Bathroom Battlegrounds and Penis Panics," *Contexts*, August 20, 2015, https://contexts.org/articles/bathroom-battlegrounds-and-penis-panics/ (accessed March 18, 2019).

27. Cunningham and Buzuvis, "Better Locker Rooms."

28. Ritch C. Savin-Williams, "A Guide to Genderqueer, Non-Binary, and Genderfluid Identity," *Psychology Today*, July 29, 2018, https://www.psychologytoday.com/us/blog/sex-sexuality-and-romance/201807/guide-genderqueer-non-binary-and-genderfluid-identity (accessed July 6, 2019).

29. Lee Airton, *Gender: Your Guide* (New York: Adams Media, 2018), 67.

30. Heather Dockray, "How the Olympics Can Embrace Non-Binary Athletes in 2020 and Beyond," Mashable, February 26, 2018, https://mashable.com/2018/02/26/olympics-non-binary-genderqueer-athletes/#6I5DFBYVHSqO (accessed March 21, 2019).

31. Ibid.

32. Schultz, *Qualifying Times*, 114.

33. Lauren Stelle, "Chris Mosier on Making History as First Trans Member of Team USA," *Rolling Stone*, August 2, 2016, https://www.rollingstone.com/culture/culture-sports/chris-mosier-on-making-history-as-first-trans-member-of-team-usa-250971/ (accessed May 6, 2019).

34. Dockray, "How the Olympics Can Embrace Non-Binary Athletes."

5. BOW OR NO BOW?

1. Michael Sotto, "Jason Collins' Coming Out Story: The Conversations, Emotions and Legacy behind His Comeback with the Nets," *The Athletic*, Febru-

ary 28, 2019, https://theathletic.com/841269/2019/02/28/jason-collins-coming-out-story-the-conversations-emotions-and-legacy-behind-his-comeback-with-the-nets/ (accessed March 25, 2019).

2. Cyd Ziegler, *Fair Play: How LGBT Athletes Are Claiming Their Rightful Place in Sports* (Brooklyn, NY: Akashic Books, 2016), 76–77.

3. Ibid., 77.

4. Susan K. Cahn, "From the 'Muscle Moll' to the 'Butch' Ballplayer: Mannishness, Lesbianism and Homophobia in U.S. Women's Sport," *Feminist Studies* 19, no. 2 (1993): 345.

5. Jaime Schultz, *Qualifying Times: Points of Change in U.S. Women's Sport* (Urbana: University of Illinois Press, 2014), 52.

6. Cahn, "From the 'Muscle Moll,'" 345–46.

7. Ibid., 346.

8. Ibid., 347.

9. Ibid., 348–49.

10. Larry Schwartz, "Didrikson Was a Woman ahead of Her Time," ESPN, n.d., https://www.espn.com/sportscentury/features/00014147.html (accessed March 27, 2019).

11. Quoted in Carolyn Gage, "Me, Babe, and Prying Open the Lesbian Closets of Women Athletes," *On the Issues Magazine*, June 28, 2012, https://www.ontheissuesmagazine.com/2012spring/cafe2.php?id=227 (accessed March 27, 2019).

12. Cahn, "From the 'Muscle Moll,'" 349.

13. Gage, "Me, Babe, and Prying Open the Lesbian Closets."

14. Laurel R. Davis-Delano, April Pollock, and Jennifer Ellsworth Vose, "Apologetic Behavior among Female Athletes," *International Review for the Sociology of Sport* 44, no. 2–3 (2009): 131.

15. After her marriage, Didrikson did live with Betty Dodd, a fellow golfer who one of Didrikson's biographers identified as her "primary partner." There's no way to know for certain if Dodd and Didrikson were romantically or sexually involved. Making assumptions about the sexual identity of historical figures who didn't themselves identify as gay or lesbian is complicated. On the one hand, making these arguments provides support for the position that same-gender love and sexuality have existed throughout history. On the other hand, our current ideas about what it means to be homosexual, gay, or lesbian are very specific to this time period and this culture. To impose these contemporary ideas on the past is to ignore how ideas about sexuality, sexual behavior, and gender have changed over time.

16. Davis-Delano et al., "Apologetic Behavior," 139–40.

17. Ibid., 142.

18. Graham Hays, "Stereotypes Haunt Softball," ESPN, October 11, 2010, http://www.espn.com/college-sports/columns/story?columnist=hays_graham& id=5671978 (accessed March 30, 2019).

19. Ibid.

20. Eric Anderson, Rory Magrath, and Rachael Bullingham, *Out in Sport: The Experiences of Openly Gay and Lesbian Athletes in Competitive Sport* (New York: Routledge, 2016), 75.

21. Harrison Smith, "Rene Portland, Penn State Basketball Coach Accused of Anti-Gay Discrimination, Dies at 65," *Washington Post*, July 23, 2018, https:// www.washingtonpost.com/local/obituaries/rene-portland-penn-state-basketball-coach-accused-of-anti-gay-discrimination-dies-at-65/2018/07/23/625993d4-8e81-11e8-8322-b5482bf5e0f5_story.html?utm_term=.be1e7bb1b20b (accessed March 30, 2019).

22. Anderson et al., *Out in Sport*, 76.

23. Ibid.

24. Ibid., 77.

25. Lonnae O'Neal, "The Struggle Is Real: The Unrelenting Weight of being a Black, Female Athlete," The Undefeated, June 25, 2018, https://theundefeated. com/features/the-struggle-is-real-the-unrelenting-weight-of-being-a-black-female-athlete/ (accessed July 7, 2019).

26. Ibid.

27. Jenny Lind Withycombe, "Intersecting Selves: African American Female Athletes Experiences of Sport," *Sociology of Sport Journal* 28 (2011): 485.

28. Geert Hekma, "'As Long as They Don't Make an Issue of It . . . ' Gay Men and Lesbians in Organized Sports in the Netherlands," *Journal of Homosexuality* 35, no. 1 (1998): 1–23; Eric Anderson, "Openly Gay Athletes: Contesting Hegemonic Masculinity in a Homophobic Environment," *Gender & Society* 16, no. 6 (2002): 860–77; Anderson et al., *Out in Sport*, 73.

29. K. L. Broad, "The Gendered Unapologetic: Queer Resistance in Women's Sports," *Sociology of Sport Journal* 18 (2001): 192–94.

30. Ibid., 194–95.

31. Nina Mandell, "WNBA Players Respond to Ex-Player's Claims That 98 Percent of the League Is Gay," *USA Today*, February 22, 2017, https://www. usatoday.com/story/sports/ftw/2017/02/22/a-former-wnba-player-said-she-was-bullied-in-a-league-filled-with-jealousy-heres-how-wnba-players-responded/ 98242446/ (accessed March 31, 2019).

32. Laurel R. Davis-Delano, "Sport as Context for the Development of Women's Same-Sex Relationships," *Journal of Sport and Social Issues* 38, no. 3 (2014): 266–67.

33. Ibid., 267.

34. Ibid., 266.

35. Jill Gutowitz, "Why Queer Women Are Obsessed with the U.S. Women's National Soccer Team," Them, June 19, 2019, https://www.them.us/story/us-womens-national-soccer-team-lesbian-visibility (accessed July 8, 2019).

36. Ibid.

6. INSIDE THE BOYS' LOCKER ROOM

1. Jason Page, "Opinion: Why Michael Sam Is a Footnote in History, Not a Trailblazer," NBCNews, 23 August 2016, https://www.nbcnews.com/feature/nbc-out/opinion-why-michael-sam-footnote-history-not-trailblazer-n634786 (accessed May 8, 2019); Jared Dubin, "Michael Sam, First Openly Gay Player, Retires for Mental Health Reasons," CBSSports, August 24, 2015, https://www.cbssports.com/nfl/news/michael-sam-first-openly-gay-player-retires-for-mental-health-reasons/ (accessed May 8, 2019).

2. Eric Anderson, Rory Magrath, and Rachael Bullingham, *Out in Sport: The Experiences of Openly Gay and Lesbian Athletes in Competitive Sport* (New York: Routledge, 2016), 24.

3. Anderson et al., *Out in Sport*, 24–25.

4. Christopher Klein, "How Teddy Roosevelt Saved Football," History Channel, September 6, 2012, https://www.history.com/news/how-teddy-roosevelt-saved-football (accessed May 8, 2019).

5. Ibid.

6. Eric Anderson, "'I Used to Think Women Were Weak': Orthodox Masculinity, Gender Segregation, and Sport," *Sociological Forum* 23, no. 2 (2008): 257–80.

7. Mary Louise Adams, *Artistic Impressions: Figure Skating, Masculinity and the Limits of Sport* (Toronto: University of Toronto Press, 2011), 82.

8. Ibid., 83.

9. Eion O'Callaghan, "Adam Rippon, John Curry, and Figure Skating's Complex History with Gay Athletes," *Guardian*, February 17, 2018, https://www.theguardian.com/sport/2018/feb/17/adam-rippon-lgbt-figure-skaters-john-curry (accessed May 9, 2018).

10. Ibid.

11. Ibid.

12. Ibid.

13. Alim Kheraj, "Ice Skating Had Its Gay Pop Moment This Year—But Things Weren't Always This Way," VICE, March 30, 2018, https://i-d.vice.com/en_uk/article/ywxw9m/ice-skating-had-its-gay-pop-moment-this-year-but-things-werent-always-this-way (accessed May 9, 2019).

14. Anderson et al., *Out in Sport*, 58.

15. Ibid., 59.

16. Eric Anderson and Mark McCormack, "Being a Black Gay Male Athlete," *Gender & Society* (blog), May 1, 2014, https://gendersociety.wordpress.com/2014/05/01/being-a-black-gay-male-athlete/ (accessed July 8, 2019).

17. D. Baunauch and E. Burgess, "Southern (Dis)comfort: Sexual Prejudice and Contact with Gay Men and Lesbians in the South," *Sociological Spectrum* 30 (2010): 30–64; L. K. Waldner, A. Sikka, and S. Baig, "Ethnicity and Sex Differences in University Students' Knowledge of AIDS, Fear of AIDS, and Attitudes Toward Gay Men," *Journal of Homosexuality* 37, no. 3 (1999): 117–33; E. G. Ward, "Homophobia, Hypermasculinity and the U.S. Black Church," *Culture, Health and Sexuality* 7, no. 5 (2007): 493–504.

18. Baunauch and Burgess, "Southern (Dis)comfort."

19. Anderson and McCormack, "Being a Black Gay Male Athlete."

20. Curtis M. Wong, "Michael Sam Says He's Been Told He's Not Gay or Black Enough," Huffpost, March 31, 2016, https://www.huffpost.com/entry/michael-sam-racism-gay-community_n_56fd38a6e4b0daf53aeee64e (accessed May 10, 2019).

21. Anderson and McCormack, "Being a Black Gay Male Athlete."

22. Eric Anderson and Mark McCormack, "Comparing the Black and Gay Male Athlete: Patterns in American Oppression," *Journal of Men's Studies* 18, no. 2 (2010): 148.

23. Jim Buzinski, "There Have Been 11 Known Gay Players in NFL History," Outsports, June 20, 2017, https://www.outsports.com/2017/6/20/15842796/gay-nfl-players-history-kopay-ocallaghan (accessed May 10, 2019).

24. Anderson et al., *Out in Sport*, 90–91.

25. Patrick Barkham, "Anton Hysen: 'Anyone Afraid of Coming Out Should Give Me a Call,'" *Guardian*, March 29, 2011, https://www.theguardian.com/football/2011/mar/29/anton-hysen-afraid-coming-out (accessed May 10, 2019).

26. Anderson et al., *Out in Sport*, 103.

27. Matias Grez, "'Impossible to Be Openly Homosexual in Football,' Says France Star Olivier Giroud," CNN, November 16, 2018, https://www.cnn.com/2018/11/16/football/olivier-giroud-football-openly-gay-players-spt-intl/index.html (accessed May 10, 2019).

28. Anderson et al., *Out in Sport*, 91.

29. Ibid., 92–93.

30. Ibid., 93.

31. Teresa Willis, "Kicking Down Barriers: Gay Footballers, Challenging Stereotypes, and Changing Attitudes in Amateur League Play," *Soccer & Society* 16, no. 2–3 (2014): 378.

32. Cyd Zeigler, *Fair Play: How LGBT Athletes Are Claiming Their Rightful Place in Sports* (Brooklyn, NY: Akashic Books, 2016).

33. Buzinski, "There Have Been 11 Known Gay Players."

34. John M. Becker, "NFL Documentary Profiles Closeted Gay Player," Bilerico Project, January 30, 2014, http://bilerico.lgbtqnation.com/2014/01/nfl_documentary_profiles_closeted_gay_player.php (accessed May 14, 2019).

35. Stuart Forward, "Gay Football Supporters Network (GFSN) League: Interview," EQVIEW, August 6, 2014, https://web.archive.org/web/20140919191533/http://eqview.com/2014/08/06/gay-football-gfsn-league-interview/ (accessed May 13, 2019).

36. "Teams," Gay Football Supporters Network, n.d., https://www.gfsn.co.uk/?page_id=614 (accessed May 13, 2019).

37. Anderson et al., *Out in Sport*, 84–85.

38. Willis, "Kicking Down Barriers," 382.

39. Ibid.

40. Andrew Schrack-Walters, Kathleen O'Donnell, and Daniel L. Wadlow, "Deconstructing the Myth of the Monolithic Male Athlete: A Qualitative Study of Men's Participation in Athletics," *Sex Roles* 60, no. 1–2 (2009): 81–99.

41. Anderson et al., *Out in Sport*, 125.

42. Ibid., 138.

7. WHY THE DUTCH ARE
SO GOOD AT BASEBALL

1. Kevin Baxter, "Curacao an Island unto Itself When It Comes to Producing Big-League Ballplayers," *Los Angeles Times*, March 26, 2018, https://www.latimes.com/sports/mlb/la-sp-baseball-curacao-20180326-story.html (accessed May 15, 2019).

2. "The History of Curacao," Curacao Travel Guide, https://www.curacao-travelguide.com/about/history/ (accessed May 16, 2019); "Curacao," *The World Factbook* (Central Intelligence Agency, 2019), https://www.cia.gov/library/publications/the-world-factbook/geos/uc.html (accessed May 16, 2019).

3. "Curacao."

4. Erin Blakemore, "What Is Colonialism?" *National Geographic Explorer*, February 19, 2019, https://www.nationalgeographic.com/culture/topics/reference/colonialism/ (accessed May 16, 2019).

5. Editors of Encyclopaedia Britannica, "Sir Ranjitsinhji Vibhaji, Maharaja Jam Sahib of Nawanagar," *Encyclopaedia Britannica*, March 29, 2019, https://www.britannica.com/biography/Sir-Ranjitsinhji-Vibhaji-Maharaja-Jam-Sahib-of-Nawanagar (accessed May 17, 2019).

6. Brian Stoddart, "Sport, Cultural Imperialism, and the Colonial Response in the British Empire," *Comparative Studies in Society and History* 30, no. 4 (1988): 655.

7. Ibid., 650–51.

8. Rugby union and rugby league both originate from the same game, beginning in England. Rugby union has teams of 15 players while rugby league has 13. For more information, see John Nauright, "Rugby," *Encyclopaedia Britannica*, n.d., https://www.britannica.com/sports/rugby (accessed July 9, 2019).

9. Stoddart, "Sport, Cultural Imperialism, and the Colonial Response," 653.

10. "It's Not Cricket," The Free Dictionary, n.d., https://idioms. thefreedictionary.com/it%27s+not+cricket (accessed May 19, 2019).

11. Stoddart, "Sport, Cultural Imperialism, and the Colonial Response," 658.

12. Ibid., 659.

13. Ibid., 655–56.

14. Richard C. Latham, "Polo," *Encyclopaedia Britannica*, n.d., https://www. britannica.com/sports/polo (accessed May 17, 2019).

15. Fabrice Delsahut, "First Nations Women, Games, and Sport in Pre- and Post-Colonial North America," *Women's History Review* 23, no. 6 (2014): 977.

16. Ibid., 980–82.

17. Ibid., 980–81.

18. Ibid., 985.

19. Ibid., 985–87.

20. Stoddart, "Sport, Cultural Imperialism, and the Colonial Response," 670.

21. Brendan Hokowhitu, "Colonized Physicality, Body Logic, and Embodied Sovereignty," in *Global Histories and Contemporary Experiences*, ed. Laura R. Graham and H. Glenn Penny (Lincoln: University of Nebraska Press, 2014), 273–89.

22. Stoddart, "Sport, Cultural Imperialism, and the Colonial Response," 667.

23. Ibid.

24. Adrian Burgos Jr., *Playing America's Game: Baseball, Latinos and the Color Line* (Berkeley: University of California Press, 2007), 18.

25. Sayuri Guthrie-Shimizu, *TransPacific Field of Dreams: How Baseball Linked the United States and Japan in Peace and War* (Chapel Hill: University of North Carolina Press, 2012), 10.

26. Ibid., 10–11.

27. Alan M. Klein, "Culture, Politics, and Baseball in the Dominican Republic," *Latin American Perspectives* 22, no. 3 (1995): 113.

28. Ibid., 114.

29. Alex Butler, "MLB: Data Shows Dramatic Decrease in Black Players, Surge in Latin Players," UPI, April 18, 2019, https://www.upi.com/Sports_

News/MLB/2019/04/18/MLB-Data-shows-dramatic-decrease-in-black-players-surge-in-Latin-players/8761555597497/ (accessed May 20, 2019).

30. Nick Said, "Meet France's World Cup Players with Deep African Roots," *Sunday Times*, July 1, 2018, https://www.timeslive.co.za/sport/soccer/2018-07-01-meet-frances-world-cup-players-with-deep-african-roots/ (accessed May 21, 2019).

31. Ibid.

32. Patrick Smith, "Soccer in the Spotlight as Europe Grapples with Racism on and off the Field," NBCNews, April 14, 2019, https://www.nbcnews.com/news/world/soccer-spotlight-europe-grapples-racism-field-n992911 (accessed May 21, 2019).

33. Ibid.

34. Burgos Jr., *Playing America's Game*, 237.

35. Ibid.

36. Ibid.

37. Ibid., 237–38.

38. Klein, "Culture, Politics, and Baseball," 115.

39. Nate Abaurrea, "It's Been 19 Years Since the MLB Played in Mexico. Christian Villanueva Is Ready to Bring It Back," SB Nation, May 3, 2018, https://www.sbnation.com/mlb/2018/5/3/17310648/mlb-en-mexico-monterrey-christian-villanueva-padres-dodgers (accessed May 22, 2019); Mike Axisa, "Mexico and Montreal Are Possible Expansion Locations as MLB Commissioner 'Would Like to Get to 32 Teams,'" CBS Sports, May 5, 2018, https://www.cbssports.com/mlb/news/mexico-and-montreal-are-possible-expansion-locations-as-mlb-commissioner-would-like-to-get-to-32-teams/ (accessed May 22, 2019).

40. "NFL Announces Five 2019 International Games," NFL.com, January 21, 2019, http://www.nfl.com/news/story/0ap3000001012392/article/nfl-announces-five-2019-international-games (accessed May 22, 2019).

41. Lou Antolihao, *Playing with the Big Boys: Basketball, American Imperialism, and Subaltern Discourse in the Philippines* (Lincoln: University of Nebraska Press, 2015), 149–50.

42. Adam Reed, "NBA Steps Up Its Global Plans to Take Basketball to New Markets," CNBC, January 18, 2019, https://www.cnbc.com/2019/01/18/nba-steps-up-its-global-plans-to-take-basketball-to-new-markets.html (accessed May 22, 2019).

8. THE BEST ITALIAN
BASEBALL PLAYER IS BLACK

1. Dave Zirin, *A People's History of Sports in the United States: 250 Years of Politics, Protest, People and Play* (New York: New Press, 2008), 101–3.

2. Ibid., 22.

3. David Reed, "High Tributes Paid to Murphy," *Lexington Herald*, May 5, 1967, http://www.uky.edu/Projects/AfricanCem/reference/ref003002.html (accessed May 24, 2019).

4. Warren Goldstein, "Unfair Play," *New York Times*, July 23, 2006, https://www.nytimes.com/2006/07/23/books/review/23goldstein.html (accessed May 24, 2019).

5. DeAngelo Starnes, "The Lost History of Black Jockeys," *American Renaissance*, June 5, 2009, https://www.amren.com/news/2009/06/the_lost_histor/ (accessed May 24, 2019).

6. Goldstein, "Unfair Play."

7. "The Mann Act," Public Broadcasting Service, n.d., https://www.pbs.org/kenburns/unforgivable-blackness/mann-act (accessed May 26, 2019).

8. Zirin, *A People's History of Sports*, 43–44.

9. "RACE: The Power of an Illusion: The Difference between Us," California Newsreel, 2003, http://newsreel.org/video/race-the-power-of-an-illusion (accessed May 26, 2019).

10. Ibid.

11. Ibid.

12. Ibid.

13. Becky Little, "The Most Controversial Census Changes in American History," History Channel, March 29, 2018, https://www.history.com/news/census-changes-controversy-citizenship (accessed May 26, 2019).

14. Jane P. Sheldon, Toby Epstein Jayaratne, and Elizabeth M. Petty, "White Americans' Genetic Explanations for a Perceived Race Difference in Athleticism: The Relation to Prejudice toward and Stereotyping of Blacks," *Athletic Insight: The Online Journal of Sport Psychology* 9, no. 3 (2007): 32.

15. James H. Frey and D. Stanley Eitzen, "Sport and Society," *Annual Review of Sociology* 17 (1991): 513; Robert E. Washington and David Karen, "Sport and Society," *Annual Review of Sociology* 27 (2001): 192.

16. Branson Wright, "The Only MLB All-Star Game That Featured Two African-American Starting Pitchers," *The Undefeated*, July 9, 2019, https://theundefeated.com/features/the-only-mlb-all-star-game-that-featured-two-african-american-starting-pitchers/ (accessed July 11, 2019).

17. Maya A. Jones, "Black Female Athletes: Things Are Better, but Far from Fair," *The Undefeated*, November 14, 2018, https://theundefeated.com/features/

black-female-athletes-morgan-state-the-undefeatedthings-are-better-but-far-from-fair/ (accessed July 11, 2019).

18. B. D. Volz, "Race and Quarterback Survival in the National Football League," *Journal of Sports Economics* 18, no. 8 (2017): 850–66.

19. Jason Reid and Jane McManus, "The NFL's Racial Divide," *The Undefeated*, n.d., https://theundefeated.com/features/the-nfls-racial-divide/ (accessed May 28, 2019); theSCOREX, "NFL Census 2017–18," Medium, July 26, 2018, https://medium.com/thescorex/nfl-census-2017-18-34223d0148a7 (accessed July 18, 2019).

20. theSCOREX, "NFL Census 2017–18."

21. Reid and McManus, "The NFL's Racial Divide."

22. Siduri J. Haslerig, Rican Vue, and Sara E. Grummert, "Invincible Bodies: American Sport Media's Racialization of Black and White College Football Players," *International Review for the Sociology of Sport* 1, no. 19 (2018): 3.

23. Reid and McManus, "The NFL's Racial Divide."

24. Evan Dent, "'Natural Athletes' vs. 'Hard Workers': What We Talk about When We Describe Athletes," *McGill Daily*, November 12, 2012, https://www.mcgilldaily.com/2012/11/natural-athletes-vs-hard-workers/ (accessed May 29, 2019).

25. Fred Segal, "Wes Welker Was a Wayne Chrebet Type Who Was a Steve Trasker Type Who Was a Steve Largent Type," Freezing Cold Takes, January 31, 2017, http://thecomeback.com/freezingcoldtakes/nfl/wes-welker-wayne-chrebet-type-steve-tasker-type-steve-largent-type.html (accessed May 29, 2019).

26. Haslerig et al., "Invincible Bodies," 2.

27. Ibid., 3.

28. Ibid.

29. Jason Silverstein, "I Don't Feel Your Pain: A Failure of Empathy Perpetuates Racial Disparities," *Slate*, June 27, 2013, https://slate.com/technology/2013/06/racial-empathy-gap-people-dont-perceive-pain-in-other-races.html (accessed May 31, 2019).

30. Maya A. Jones, "New Study Examines History of Black Women Fighting to Be Respected as Athletes," *The Undefeated*, June 25, 2018, https://theundefeated.com/features/morgan-state-university-study-examines-history-of-black-women-fighting-to-be-respected-as-athletes/ (accessed July 12, 2019).

31. Julee Wilson, "Haters Attack Gabby Douglas' Hair Again and Twitter Promptly Claps Back," *Essence*, August 8, 2016, https://www.essence.com/news/gabby-douglas-hair-haters-twitter-claps-back/ (accessed July 12, 2019).

32. Jones, "New Study Examines History of Black Women."

33. Sopan Deb, "Ibtihaj Muhammad: The Olympic Fencer Is Charting Her Own Path," *New York Times*, July 24, 2018, https://www.nytimes.com/2018/07/

24/books/ibtihaj-muhammad-fencing-hijab-olympics.html (accessed July 12, 2019).

34. "Unapologetic: The Black Female Athlete," *The Undefeated*, February 24, 2018, https://theundefeated.com/videos/unapologetic-the-black-female-athlete-2/ (accessed July 12, 2019).

35. Nikole Tower, "In an Ethnic Breakdown of Sports, NBA Takes Lead for Most Diverse," GlobalSportMatters, https://globalsportmatters.com/culture/2018/12/12/in-an-ethnic-breakdown-of-sports-nba-takes-lead-for-most-diverse/ (accessed May 29, 2019).

36. Lisa Wade, "When Jews Dominated Professional Basketball," Sociological Images, November 25, 2013, https://thesocietypages.org/socimages/2013/11/25/when-jews-dominated-professional-basketball/ (accessed May 29, 2019).

37. Ibid.

38. Zirin, *A People's History of Sports*, 43.

39. "Odds of a High School Female Athlete Going Pro," Scholarship-Stats.com, n.d., http://www.scholarshipstats.com/odds-of-going-pro-women.htm (accessed July 12, 2019).

40. "Estimated Probability of Competing in Professional Athletics," NCAA, n.d., http://www.ncaa.org/about/resources/research/estimated-probability-competing-professional-athletics (accessed May 29, 2019).

41. J. J. Cooper, "How Many MLB Draftees Make It to the Majors," Baseball America, May 17, 2019, https://www.baseballamerica.com/stories/how-many-mlb-draftees-make-it-to-the-majors/ (accessed May 29, 2019).

42. Richard Lapchick, "The 2018 Racial and Gender Report Card: National Football League," Institute for Diversity and Ethics in Sports, April 15, 2019, https://docs.wixstatic.com/ugd/7d86e5_0fea53798fdf472289 d0966a8b009d6c.pdf (accessed May 30, 2019).

43. Richard Lapchick, "The 2018 Racial and Gender Report Card: National Basketball Association," Institute for Diversity and Ethics in Sports, June 26, 2018, http://nebula.wsimg.com/b10c21a67a6d1035091c4e5784c012f4? AccessKeyId=DAC3A56D8FB782449D2A&disposition=0&alloworigin=1 (accessed May 30, 2019).

44. The NBA also exceeds other leagues in gender representation in its league offices, with 39.6 percent women compared to 35 percent in the NFL and 30.8 in MLB.

45. "NFL Expands Rooney Rule Requirements to Strengthen Diversity," NFL.com, December 12, 2018, http://www.nfl.com/news/story/0ap3000000999110/article/nfl-expands-rooney-rule-requirements-to-strengthen-diversity (accessed May 30, 2019).

46. Seth Abrahamson, "Does the Rooney Rule Work?" *Spectator*, March 6, 2018, https://www.spectatornews.com/sports/2018/03/06/does-the-rooney-rule-work/ (accessed May 30, 2019).

47. Luke Knox, "NFL Hires in the Rooney Rule Era," *The Undefeated*, n.d., https://theundefeated.com/features/nfl-hires-in-the-rooney-rule-era/ (accessed May 30, 2019).

48. Derek Jeter, retired Yankees shortstop, is part owner of the Miami Marlins and serves as the team's CEO.

49. Stacy Jones, "White Men Account for 72% of Corporate Leadership at 16 of the Fortune 500 Companies," *Fortune*, June 9, 2017, http://fortune.com/2017/06/09/white-men-senior-executives-fortune-500-companies-diversity-data/ (accessed May 30, 2019).

50. Brent Schrotenboer, "How NFL Owners Trip over Themselves Despite Wealth, Power," *USA Today*, March 28, 2019, https://www.usatoday.com/story/sports/nfl/2019/03/28/nfl-owners-wealth-cant-keep-them-out-trouble/3281774002/ (accessed May 30, 2019).

51. Amy Held, "Controversial Serena Williams Cartoon Ruled 'Non-Racist' by Australia's Press Council," National Public Radio, February 25, 2019, https://www.npr.org/2019/02/25/697672690/controversial-serena-cartoon-ruled-non-racist-by-australia-s-governing-press-bod (accessed July 12, 2019).

9. RIDING A BIKE, RAISING A FIST, AND TAKING A KNEE

1. J. R. Thorpe, "The Feminist History of Bicycles," *Bustle*, May 12, 2017, https://www.bustle.com/p/the-feminist-history-of-bicycles-57455 (accessed June 3, 2019).

2. Ibid.

3. Ibid.

4. Ibid.

5. M. B. Roberts, "Rudolph Ran and World Went Wild," ESPN, https://www.espn.com/sportscentury/features/00016444.html (accessed June 4, 2019); "On the Shoulders of Giants," National Public Radio, February 14, 2019, https://www.npr.org/templates/transcript/transcript.php?storyId=693878396 (accessed June 4, 2019).

6. "On the Shoulders of Giants."

7. Ibid.

8. Ibid.

9. Larry Schwartz, "Billie Jean Won for All Women," ESPN, n.d., https://www.espn.com/sportscentury/features/00016060.html (accessed June 5, 2019).

10. "Reserve Clause," Baseball Reference, n.d., https://www.baseball-reference.com/bullpen/Reserve_clause (accessed June 5, 2019).

11. Dave Zirin, *A People's History of Sports: 250 Years of Politics, Protest, People and Play* (New York: New Press, 2008), 205–6.

12. Zirin, *A People's History of Sports*, 206; "50 Years Later: Curt Flood's Historic Sacrifice for Fellow Players," Major League Baseball Players, n.d., http://www.mlbplayers.com/ViewArticle.dbml?DB_OEM_ID=34000& ATCLID=211460114 (accessed June 5, 2019).

13. "50 Years Later."

14. Zirin, *A People's History of Sports*, 206.

15. "Report: MLB Revenues Exceed $10 Billion for the First Time," *USA Today*, November 22, 2017, https://www.usatoday.com/story/sports/mlb/2017/11/22/mlb-revenues-exceed-10-billion/890041001/ (accessed June 5, 2019).

16. Nat Berman, "The 20 Richest MLB Owners in the World," *Money, Inc.*, 2018, https://moneyinc.com/the-20-richest-mlb-owners-in-the-world/ (accessed June 5, 2019).

17. Lori Weisberg, "Is Owning a Baseball Team a Money Maker?" *San Diego Union Tribune*, August 7, 2012, https://www.sandiegouniontribune.com/sports/padres/sdut-owning-a-baseball-team-rarely-a-losing-proposition-2012aug07-story.html (accessed June 5, 2019).

18. Maury Brown, "MLB Spent Less on Player Salaries Despite Record Revenues in 2018," *Forbes*, January 11, 2019, https://www.forbes.com/sites/maurybrown/2019/01/11/economic-data-shows-mlb-spent-less-on-player-salaries-compared-to-revenues-in-2018/#2996b4b639d7 (accessed June 5, 2019).

19. Kareem Abdul-Jabbar, "College Athletes of the World, Unite," Jacobin, November 12, 2014, https://www.jacobinmag.com/2014/11/college-athletes-of-the-world-unite/ (accessed June 5, 2019).

20. Karen Given and Shira Springer, "Before Kaepernick, The 'Syracuse 8' Were Blackballed by Pro Football," WBUR, November 17, 2017, https://www.wbur.org/onlyagame/2017/11/17/syracuse-8-football-boycott-kaepernick (accessed June 6, 2019).

21. Ibid.

22. Ibid.

23. Rohan Nodkarni and Alex Nieves, "Why Missouri's Football Team Joined a Protest against School Administration," *Sports Illustrated*, November 9, 2015, https://www.si.com/college-football/2015/11/09/missouri-football-protest-racism-tim-wolfe (accessed June 6, 2019).

24. Jesse Washington, "Still No Anthem, Still No Regrets for Mahmoud Abdul-Raud," *The Undefeated*, September 1, 2016, https://theundefeated.com/

features/abdul-rauf-doesnt-regret-sitting-out-national-anthem/ (accessed June 7, 2019).

25. Steve Heisler, "Former Chicago Bulls Guard Craig Hodges Was Dropped in 1992 for Suspicious Reasons," *Chicago Reader*, June 4, 2018, https://www.chicagoreader.com/Bleader/archives/2018/06/04/former-chicago-bulls-guard-craig-hodges-was-dropped-in-1992-for-suspicious-reasons (accessed June 7, 2019).

26. Kathy Kudravi, "Republicans Buy Sneakers, Too: Athlete Activism Is on the Rise, but So Is the Backlash," GlobalSportMatters, April 26, 2018, https://globalsportmatters.com/tag/republicans-buy-sneakers-too/ (accessed June 7, 2019).

27. Ibid.

28. William C. Rhoden, "Major League Baseball Struck Out at the World Series by Not Facing Up to Blatant Racism," *The Undefeated*, November 2, 2017, https://theundefeated.com/features/major-league-baseball-struck-out-at-the-world-series-by-not-facing-up-to-blatant-racism/ (accessed June 7, 2019).

29. Dave Zirin, "Nick Bosa and the NFL's Double Standards," Edge of Sports, April 27, 2019, https://www.edgeofsports.com/2019-04-27-1432/index.html (accessed June 7, 2019).

30. Julie Kliegman, "Nothing and Everything Has Changed for the USWNT," The Ringer, June 10, 2019, https://www.theringer.com/soccer/2019/6/10/18656696/us-womens-national-team-world-cup-lawsuit-1999-megan-rapinoe (accessed July 15, 2019).

31. Jerry Bembry, "The Year of Athletes and Activism," *The Undefeated*, December 29, 2017, https://theundefeated.com/features/2017-the-year-of-athletes-and-activism/ (accessed July 15, 2019).

BIBLIOGRAPHY

Abaurrea, Nate. "It's Been 19 Years since the MLB Played in Mexico. Christian Villanueva Is Ready to Bring It Back." SB Nation, May 3, 2018. https://www.sbnation.com/mlb/2018/5/3/17310648/mlb-en-mexico-monterrey-christian-villanueva-padres-dodgers (accessed May 22, 2019).

Abbott, Gary. "High School Girls Wrestling Continues Rapid Growth." National Wrestling Hall of Fame, n.d. https://nwhof.org/blog/high-school-girls-wrestling-continues-rapid-growth/ (accessed March 3, 2019).

Abdul-Jabbar, Kareem. "College Athletes of the World, Unite." Jacobin, November 12, 2014. https://www.jacobinmag.com/2014/11/college-athletes-of-the-world-unite/ (accessed June 5, 2019).

Abrahamson, Seth. "Does the Rooney Rule Work?" Spectator, March 6, 2018. https://www.spectatornews.com/sports/2018/03/06/does-the-rooney-rule-work/ (accessed May 30, 2019).

Adams, Mary Louise. Artistic Impressions: Figure Skating, Masculinity and the Limits of Sport. Toronto: University of Toronto Press, 2011.

Airton, Lee. Gender: Your Guide. New York: Adams Media, 2018.

Anderson, Eric. "'I Used to Think Women Were Weak': Orthodox Masculinity, Gender Segregation, and Sport." Sociological Forum 23, no. 2 (2008): 257–80.

Anderson, Eric. "Openly Gay Athletes: Contesting Hegemonic Masculinity in a Homophobic Environment." Gender & Society 16, no. 6 (2002): 860–77.

Anderson, Eric, Rory Magrath, and Rachael Bullingham. Out in Sport: The Experiences of Openly Gay and Lesbian Athletes in Competitive Sport. New York: Routledge, 2016.

Anderson, Eric, and Mark McCormack. "Being a Black Gay Male Athlete." Gender & Society (blog), May 1, 2014. https://gendersociety.wordpress.com/2014/05/01/being-a-black-gay-male-athlete/ (accessed July 8, 2019).

Anderson, Eric, and Mark McCormack. "Comparing the Black and Gay Male Athlete: Patterns in American Oppression." Journal of Men's Studies 18, no. 2 (2010): 145–58.

Anderson, Leigh C. "U.S. Men's Soccer Fails to Qualify for World Cup, Still Paid More Than Our Champion Women's Team." Salon, October 11, 2017. https://www.salon.com/2017/10/11/usmnt-world-cup-uswnt/ (accessed March 7, 2019).

"Androgen Insensitivity Syndrome (AIS)." Intersex Society of North America, n.d. http://www.isna.org/faq/conditions/ais (accessed February 8, 2019).

Antolihao, Lou. Playing with the Big Boys: Basketball, American Imperialism, and Subaltern Discourse in the Philippines. Lincoln: University of Nebraska Press, 2015.

Attn: Twitter post, June 21, 2019, 7:00 p.m. https://twitter.com/attn/status/1142205555374608384 (accessed July 6, 2019).

Axisa, Mike. "Mexico and Montreal Are Possible Expansion Locations as MLB Commissioner 'Would Like to Get to 32 Teams.'" CBS Sports, May 5, 2018. https://www.cbssports.com/mlb/news/mexico-and-montreal-are-possible-expansion-locations-as-mlb-commissioner-would-like-to-get-to-32-teams/ (accessed May 22, 2019).

Bailey, R., I. Wellard, and H. Dismore. "Girls' Participation in Physical Activities and Sports: Benefits, Patterns, Influences, and Ways Forward," World Health Organization, n.d. https://www.icsspe.org/sites/default/files/Girls.pdf (accessed March 4, 2019).

Barajas, Joshua. "Equal Pay for Equal Play: What the Sport of Tennis Got Right." PBS News-Hour, April 12, 2016. https://www.pbs.org/newshour/economy/equal-pay-for-equal-play-what-the-sport-of-tennis-got-right (accessed March 7, 2019).

Barkham, Patrick. "Anton Hysen: 'Anyone Afraid of Coming Out Should Give Me a Call.'" Guardian, March 29, 2011. https://www.theguardian.com/football/2011/mar/29/anton-hysen-afraid-coming-out (accessed May 10, 2019).

Baunauch, D., and E. Burgess. "Southern (Dis)comfort: Sexual Prejudice and Contact with Gay Men and Lesbians in the South." Sociological Spectrum, 30 (2010): 30–64.

Baxter, Kevin. "Curacao an Island unto Itself When It Comes to Producing Big-League Ball-players." Los Angeles Times, March 26, 2018. https://www.latimes.com/sports/mlb/la-sp-baseball-curacao-20180326-story.html (accessed May 15, 2019).

Becker, John M. "NFL Documentary Profiles Closeted Gay Player." Bilerico Project, January 30, 2014. http://bilerico.lgbtqnation.com/2014/01/nfl_documentary_profiles_closeted_gay_player.php (accessed May 14, 2019).

Bembry, Jerry. "The Year of Athletes and Activism." The Undefeated, December 29, 2017. https://theundefeated.com/features/2017-the-year-of-athletes-and-activism/ (accessed July 15, 2019).

Berman, Nat. "The 20 Richest MLB Owners in the World." Money, Inc., 2018. https://moneyinc.com/the-20-richest-mlb-owners-in-the-world/ (accessed June 5, 2019).

Berri, David. "Basketball's Growing Gender Wage Gap: The Evidence the WNBA Is Under-paying Players." Forbes, September 20, 2017. https://www.forbes.com/sites/davidberri/2017/09/20/there-is-a-growing-gender-wage-gap-in-professional-basketball/#4fb7664d36e0 (accessed March 7, 2019).

Bhasin, Shalender, Thomas W. Storer, Nancy Berman, Carlos Callegari, Brenda Clevenger, Jeffrey Phillips, Thomas J. Bunnell, Ray Tricker, Aida Shirazi, and Richard Casaburi. "The Effects of Supraphysiologic Doses of Testosterone on Muscle Size and Strength in Normal Men." New England Journal of Medicine 335, no. 1 (1996): 1–7.

Blakemore, Erin. "What Is Colonialism?" National Geographic Explorer, February 19, 2019. https://www.nationalgeographic.com/culture/topics/reference/colonialism/ (accessed May 16, 2019).

Blumenthal, Karen. Let Me Play: The Story of Title IX, the Law That Changed the Future of Girls in America. New York: Atheneum Books, 2005.

Briggs, Simon. "Why Tennis's Renee Richards, the First Transgender Woman to Play Profes-sional Sport, Matters Today." Telegraph, March 30, 2018. https://www.telegraph.co.uk/tennis/2018/03/30/tennisrenee-richards-first-transgender-woman-play-professional/ (accessed March 13, 2019).

Broad, K. L. "The Gendered Unapologetic: Queer Resistance in Women's Sports." Sociology of Sport Journal 18 (2001): 181–204.

Brown, Maury. "MLB Spent Less on Player Salaries Despite Record Revenues in 2018." Forbes, January 11, 2019. https://www.forbes.com/sites/maurybrown/2019/01/11/economic-data-shows-mlb-spent-less-on-player-salaries-compared-to-revenues-in-2018/#2996b4b639d7 (accessed June 5, 2019).

Burgos, Jr., Adrian. Playing America's Game: Baseball, Latinos and the Color Line. Berkeley: University of California Press, 2007.

Butler, Alex. "MLB: Data Shows Dramatic Decrease in Black Players, Surge in Latin Players." UPI, April 18, 2019. https://www.upi.com/Sports_News/MLB/2019/04/18/MLB-Data-shows-dramatic-decrease-in-black-players-surge-in-Latin-players/8761555597497/ (accessed May 20, 2019).

Buzinski, Jim. "There Have Been 11 Known Gay Players in NFL History." Outsports, June 20, 2017. https://www.outsports.com/2017/6/20/15842796/gay-nfl-players-history-kopay-ocallaghan (accessed May 10, 2019).

Cahn, Susan K. "From the 'Muscle Moll' to the 'Butch' Ballplayer: Mannishness, Lesbianism and Homophobia in U.S. Women's Sport." Feminist Studies 19, no. 2 (1993): 343–68.

Capranica, Laura, Maria Francesca Piacentini, Shona Halson, Kathryn H. Myburgh, Etsuko Ogasawara, and Mindy Millard-Stafford. "The Gender Gap in Sports Performance: Equity Influences Equality." International Journal of Sports Physiology and Performance 8 (2013): 99–103.

Cauterucci, Christina. "The U.S. Women's Soccer Team Finally Has a Better Contract, But Not Equal Pay." Slate, April 5, 2017. https://slate.com/human-interest/2017/04/the-u-s-womens-soccer-team-finally-has-a-better-contract-but-not-equal-pay.html (accessed March 7, 2019).

Chaffee, Ian. "Forget about Sexism: Now TV Coverage of Women's Sports Is Just Plain Boring." USCNews, September 12, 2017. https://news.usc.edu/127695/forget-about-sexism-now-tv-coverage-of-womens-sports-is-just-plain-boring/ (accessed March 8, 2019).

Chan, Kristina. "The Mother of Title IX: Patsy Mink." The She Network, April 24, 2012. https://www.womenssportsfoundation.org/education/mother-title-ix-patsy-mink/ (accessed February 13, 2019).

"Childrens' Engagement with the Outdoors and Sports Activities, UK, 2014–2015." Office for National Statistics (UK), January 30, 2018. https://www.ons.gov.uk/peoplepopulationandcommunity/wellbeing/articles/childrensengagementwiththeoutdoorsandsportsactivitiesuk/2014to2015 (accessed March 4, 2019).

Clemmons, Anna Katherine. "7 Feet 7 and 360 Pounds with Bigger Feet Than Shaq's," New York Times, January 9, 2008. https://www.nytimes.com/2008/01/09/sports/ncaabasketball/09asheville.html (accessed February 17, 2019).

Cook, Bob. "Why Girls Are the Best Hope to Save Wrestling." Forbes, February 17, 2012. https://www.forbes.com/sites/bobcook/2012/02/17/why-girls-are-the-best-hope-to-save-wrestling/#3b115f336ae9 (accessed March 3, 2019).

Cooper, J. J. "How Many MLB Draftees Make It to the Majors." Baseball America, May 17, 2019. https://www.baseballamerica.com/stories/how-many-mlb-draftees-make-it-to-the-majors/ (accessed May 29, 2019).

Cunningham, George B., and Erin E. Buzuvis. "Better Locker Rooms: It's Not Just a Transgender Thing." The Conversation, March 26, 2017. http://theconversation.com/better-locker-rooms-its-not-just-a-transgender-thing-74023 (accessed March 18, 2019).

"Curacao." The World Factbook. Central Intelligence Agency, 2019. https://www.cia.gov/library/publications/the-world-factbook/geos/uc.html (accessed May 16, 2019).

Dahl, Melissa. "The Obscure Ultra-Endurance Sport Women Are Quietly Dominating." The Cut, September 11, 2016. https://www.thecut.com/2016/09/the-obscure-endurance-sport-women-are-quietly-dominating.html (accessed March 3, 2019).

"Danica Patrick and the Women of NASCAR." ABCNews, n.d. https://abcnews.go.com/Business/photos/women-nascar-danica-patrick-indy-500-14343965/image-19000228 (accessed February 5, 2019).

Davis-Delano, Laurel R. "Sport as Context for the Development of Women's Same-Sex Relationships." Journal of Sport and Social Issues 38, no. 3 (2014): 263–85.

Davis-Delano, Laurel R., April Pollock, and Jennifer Ellsworth Vose. "Apologetic Behavior among Female Athletes." International Review for the Sociology of Sport 44, no. 2–3 (2009): 131–50.

de Oliveria, Tania Ferreira, Maria Gouveia, and Rui F. Oliveria. "Testosterone Responsiveness to Winning and Losing Experiences in Female Soccer Players." Psychoneuroendocrinology 34, no. 7 (2009): 1056–64.

Deb, Sopan. "Ibtihaj Muhammad: The Olympic Fencer Is Charting Her Own Path." New York Times, July 24, 2018. https://www.nytimes.com/2018/07/24/books/ibtihaj-muhammad-fencing-hijab-olympics.html (accessed July 12, 2019).

Debucquoy-Dodley, Dominique. "NJ Youth Basketball Team Forfeits, Won't Play Season without Girl Teammates." CNN, February 16, 2017. https://www.cnn.com/2017/02/13/us/kid-basketball-season-trnd/index.html (accessed February 13, 2019).

Delsahut, Fabrice. "First Nations Women, Games, and Sport in Pre- and Post-Colonial North America." *Women's History Review* 23, no. 6 (2014): 976–95.

Dent, Evan. "'Natural Athletes' vs. 'Hard Workers': What We Talk about When We Describe Athletes." *McGill Daily*, November 12, 2012. https://www.mcgilldaily.com/2012/11/natural-athletes-vs-hard-workers/ (accessed May 29, 2019).

"Do You Know the Factors Influencing Girls' Participation in Sports?" Women's Sports Foundation, September 9, 2016. https://www.womenssportsfoundation.org/support-us/do-you-know-the-factors-influencing-girls-participation-in-sports/ (accessed March 5, 2019).

Dockray, Heather. "How the Olympics Can Embrace Non-Binary Athletes in 2020 and Beyond." Mashable, February 26, 2018. https://mashable.com/2018/02/26/olympics-non-binary-genderqueer-athletes/#6I5DFBYVHSqO (accessed March 21, 2019).

Doyle, Jessica Ryen. "Michael Phelps Unintentionally Raises Marfan Syndrome Awareness." Foxnews.com, August 21, 2008. https://www.foxnews.com/story/michael-phelps-unintentionally-raises-marfan-syndrome-awareness (accessed February 17, 2019).

Dubin, Jared. "Michael Sam, First Openly Gay Player, Retires for Mental Health Reasons." CBSSports, August 24, 2015. https://www.cbssports.com/nfl/news/michael-sam-first-openly-gay-player-retires-for-mental-health-reasons/ (accessed May 8, 2019).

Editors of Encyclopaedia Britannica. "Sir Ranjitsinhji Vibhaji, Maharaja Jam Sahib of Nawanagar." *Encyclopaedia Britannica*, March 29, 2019. https://www.britannica.com/biography/Sir-Ranjitsinhji-Vibhaji-Maharaja-Jam-Sahib-of-Nawanagar (accessed May 17, 2019).

"Estimated Probability of Competing in Professional Athletics." NCAA, n.d. http://www.ncaa.org/about/resources/research/estimated-probability-competing-professional-athletics (accessed May 29, 2019).

Eynon, Nir, Ruth Birk, Yoav Meckel, Alejandro Lucia, Dan Nemet, and Alon Eliakim. "Physiological Variables and Mitochondrial-Related Genotypes of an Athlete Who Excels in Both Short and Long-Distance Running." *Mitochondrian* 11, no. 5 (2011): 774–77.

Eynon, Nir, Maria Moran, Ruth Birk, and Alejandro Lucia. "The Champions' Mitochondria: Is It Genetically Determined? A Review on Mitochondrial DNA and Elite Athletic Performance." *Physiological Genomics* 43, no. 13 (2011): 789–98.

Fader, Mirin. "Andraya Yearwood Knows She Has the Right to Compete." Bleacher Report, December 17, 2018. https://bleacherreport.com/articles/2810857-andraya-yearwood-knows-she-has-the-right-to-compete (accessed March 20, 2019).

Fausto-Sterling, Anne. "Gender & Sexuality." Fields of Inquiry, n.d. http://www.annefaustosterling.com/fields-of-inquiry/gender/ (accessed February 14, 2019).

"50 Years Later: Curt Flood's Historic Sacrifice for Fellow Players." Major League Baseball Players, n.d. http://www.mlbplayers.com/ViewArticle.dbml?DB_OEM_ID=34000&ATCLID=211460114 (accessed June 5, 2019).

Forward, Stuart. "Gay Football Supporters Network (GFSN) League: Interview." EQVIEW, August 6, 2014. https://web.archive.org/web/20140919191533/http://eqview.com/2014/08/06/gay-football-gfsn-league-interview/ (accessed May 13, 2019).

Francis, Bill. "League of Women Ballplayers." National Baseball Hall of Fame, n.d. https://baseballhall.org/discover-more/stories/baseball-history/league-of-women-ballplayers (accessed February 5, 2019).

Frey, James H., and D. Stanley Eitzen. "Sport and Society." *Annual Review of Sociology* 17 (1991): 503–22.

Gage, Carolyn. "Me, Babe, and Prying Open the Lesbian Closets of Women Athletes." *On the Issues Magazine*, June 28, 2012. https://www.ontheissuesmagazine.com/2012spring/cafe2.php?id=227 (accessed March 27, 2019).

"Getting More Girls in the Game of Soccer," Adidas.com, June 2019. https://www.adidas.com/us/blog/377303 (accessed July 6, 2019).

Given, Karen, and Shira Springer. "Before Kaepernick, The 'Syracuse 8' Were Blackballed by Pro Football." WBUR, November 17, 2017. https://www.wbur.org/onlyagame/2017/11/17/syracuse-8-football-boycott-kaepernick (accessed June 6, 2019).

Goldschmied, Nadav, and Jason Kowalczyck. "Gender Performance in the NCAA Rifle Championships: Where Is the Gap?" *Sex Roles* 74 (2014): 310–22.

Goldstein, Warren. "Unfair Play." *New York Times*, July 23, 2006. https://www.nytimes.com/2006/07/23/books/review/23goldstein.html (accessed May 24, 2019).

Gordon, Sherry Mabron. *Women Athletes*. Berkeley Heights, NJ: Enslow, 2017.

Grez, Matias. "'Impossible to Be Openly Homosexual in Football,' Says France Star Olivier Giroud." CNN, November 16, 2018. https://www.cnn.com/2018/11/16/football/olivier-giroud-football-openly-gay-players-spt-intl/index.html (accessed May 10, 2019).

Griffin, Pat. "Developing Policies for Transgender Students on High School Teams." National Federation of State High School Associations, September 28, 2015. http://www.nfhs.org/articles/developing-policies-for-transgender-students-on-high-school-teams/ (accessed March 15, 2019).

Gustin, Georgina. "The Olympic Committee Says Trans Athletes Can Compete without Reassignment Surgery." Medium, January 25, 2016. https://timeline.com/the-international-olympic-committee-has-nixed-the-requirement-that-transgender-athletes-have-e59a82b9e67c (accessed May 10, 2019).

Guthrie-Shimizu, Sayuri. *TransPacific Field of Dreams: How Baseball Linked the United States and Japan in Peace and War*. Chapel Hill: University of North Carolina Press, 2012.

Gutowitz, Jill. "Why Queer Women Are Obsessed with the U.S. Women's National Soccer Team." Them, June 19, 2019. https://www.them.us/story/us-womens-national-soccer-team-lesbian-visibility (accessed July 8, 2019).

Haslerig, Siduri J., Rican Vue, and Sara E. Grummert. "Invincible Bodies: American Sport Media's Racialization of Black and White College Football Players." *International Review for the Sociology of Sport* 1, no. 19 (2018): 1–17.

Hays, Graham. "Stereotypes Haunt Softball." ESPN, October 11, 2010. http://www.espn.com/college-sports/columns/story?columnist=hays_graham&id=5671978 (accessed March 30, 2019).

Heisler, Steve. "Former Chicago Bulls Guard Craig Hodges Was Dropped in 1992 for Suspicious Reasons." *Chicago Reader*, June 4, 2018. https://www.chicagoreader.com/Bleader/archives/2018/06/04/former-chicago-bulls-guard-craig-hodges-was-dropped-in-1992-for-suspicious-reasons (accessed June 7, 2019).

Hekma, Geert. "'As Long as They Don't Make an Issue of It . . . ' Gay Men and Lesbians in Organized Sports in the Netherlands." *Journal of Homosexuality* 35, no. 1 (1998): 1–23.

Held, Amy. "Controversial Serena Williams Cartoon Ruled 'Non-Racist' by Australia's Press Council." National Public Radio, February 25, 2019. https://www.npr.org/2019/02/25/697672690/controversial-serena-cartoon-ruled-non-racist-by-australia-s-governing-press-bod (accessed July 12, 2019).

"The History of Curacao." Curacao Travel Guide, n.d. https://www.curacao-travelguide.com/about/history/ (accessed May 16, 2019).

"A History of Women in Formula One." CNN Sports, August 21, 2018. https://www.cnn.com/2018/08/21/motorsport/gallery/women-in-formula-one-spt-intl/index.html (accessed February 5, 2019).

Hokowhitu, Brendan. "Colonized Physicality, Body Logic, and Embodied Sovereignty." In *Global Histories and Contemporary Experiences*, edited by Laura R. Graham and H. Glenn Penny, 273–89. Lincoln: University of Nebraska Press, 2014.

Iannelli, Vincent. "What Is the Average Height for an Adult Woman?" VeryWellFit, October 25, 2018. https://www.verywellfit.com/average-height-for-a-woman-statistics-2632136 (accessed February 21, 2019).

Ingle, Sean. "Caster Semenya Accuses IAAF of Using Her as a 'Guinea Pig Experiment.'" *Guardian*, June 18, 2019. https://www.theguardian.com/sport/2019/jun/18/caster-semenya-iaaf-athletics-guinea-pig (accessed July 5, 2019).

"IOC Rules Transgender Athletes Can Take Part in Olympics without Surgery." *Guardian*, January 24, 2016. https://www.theguardian.com/sport/2016/jan/25/ioc-rules-transgender-athletes-can-take-part-in-olympics-without-surgery (accessed March 14, 2019).

"It's Not Cricket." The Free Dictionary, n.d. https://idioms.thefreedictionary.com/it%27s+not+cricket (accessed May 19, 2019).

Jenkins, Sally. "History of Women's Basketball." WNBA, July 3, 1997. https://www.wnba.com/news/history-of-womens-basketball/ (accessed February 5, 2019).

Jones, Maya A. "Black Female Athletes: Things Are Better, but Far from Fair." *The Undefeated*, November 14, 2018. https://theundefeated.com/features/black-female-athletes-morgan-state-the-undefeatedthings-are-better-but-far-from-fair/ (accessed July 11, 2019).

Jones, Maya A. "New Study Examines History of Black Women Fighting to Be Respected as Athletes." *The Undefeated*, June 25, 2018. https://theundefeated.com/features/morgan-state-university-study-examines-history-of-black-women-fighting-to-be-respected-as-athletes/ (accessed July 12, 2019).

Jones, Stacy. "White Men Account for 72% of Corporate Leadership at 16 of the Fortune 500 Companies." *Fortune*, June 9, 2017. http://fortune.com/2017/06/09/white-men-senior-executives-fortune-500-companies-diversity-data/ (accessed May 30, 2019).

"K–12 Policies." Transathlete, n.d. https://www.transathlete.com/k-12 (accessed March 15, 2019).

Karkazis, Katrina. "The Testosterone Myth." *Wired*, March 27, 2018. https://www.wired.com/story/testosterone-treatment-myth/ (accessed February 14, 2019).

Karkazis, Katrina, Rebecca Jordan-Young, Georgiann Davis, and Silvia Camporesi. "Out of Bounds? A Critique of the New Policies on Hyperandrogenism in Elite Female Athletes." *American Journal of Bioethics* 12, no. 7 (2012): 3–16.

Kelley, Bruce, and Carl Carchia. "'Hey, Data Data—Swing!'" ESPN, July 11, 2013. http://www.espn.com/espn/story/_/id/9469252/hidden-demographics-youth-sports-espn-magazine (accessed March 4, 2019).

Kheraj, Alim. "Ice Skating Had Its Gay Pop Moment This Year—But Things Weren't Always This Way." VICE, March 30, 2018. https://i-d.vice.com/en_uk/article/ywxw9m/ice-skating-had-its-gay-pop-moment-this-year-but-things-werent-always-this-way (accessed May 9, 2019).

Klein, Alan M. "Culture, Politics, and Baseball in the Dominican Republic." *Latin American Perspectives* 22, no. 3 (1995): 111–30.

Klein, Christopher. "How Teddy Roosevelt Saved Football." History Channel, September 6, 2012. https://www.history.com/news/how-teddy-roosevelt-saved-football (accessed May 8, 2019).

Kliegman, Julie. "Nothing and Everything Has Changed for the USWNT." The Ringer, June 10, 2019. https://www.theringer.com/soccer/2019/6/10/18656696/us-womens-national-team-world-cup-lawsuit-1999-megan-rapinoe (accessed July 6, 2019).

"Klinefelter Syndrome." Intersex Society of North America, n.d. http://www.isna.org/faq/conditions/klinefelter (accessed February 8, 2019).

Knox, Luke. "NFL Hires in the Rooney Rule Era." *The Undefeated*, n.d., https://theundefeated.com/features/nfl-hires-in-the-rooney-rule-era/ (accessed May 30, 2019).

Kornei, Katherine. "This Scientist Is Racing to Discover How Gender Transitions Alter Athletic Performance—Including Her Own." *Science*, June 25, 2018. https://www.sciencemag.org/news/2018/07/scientist-racing-discover-how-gender-transitions-alter-athletic-performance-including (accessed July 15, 2019).

Kudravi, Kathy. "Republicans Buy Sneakers, Too: Athlete Activism Is on the Rise, but So Is the Backlash." GlobalSportMatters, April 26, 2018. https://globalsportmatters.com/tag/republicans-buy-sneakers-too/ (accessed June 7, 2019).

Laby, Daniel M., John L. Davidson, Louis J. Rosenbaum, Charles Strasser, Michael F. Mellman, Arthur L. Rosenbaum, and David G. Kirschen. "The Visual Function of Professional Baseball Players." *American Journal of Opthalmology* 122, no. 4 (1996): 476–85.

Lapchick, Richard. "The 2018 Racial and Gender Report Card: National Basketball Association." The Institute for Diversity and Ethics in Sports, June 26, 2018. http://nebula.wsimg.com/b10c21a67a6d1035091c4e5784c012f4?AccessKeyId=DAC3A56D8FB782449D2A&disposition=0&alloworigin=1 (accessed May 30, 2019).

Lapchick, Richard. "The 2018 Racial and Gender Report Card: National Football League." Institute for Diversity and Ethics in Sports, April 15, 2019. https://docs.wixstatic.com/ugd/7d86e5_0fea53798fdf472289d0966a8b009d6c.pdf (accessed May 30, 2019).

Latham, Richard C. "Polo." *Encyclopaedia Britannica*, n.d. https://www.britannica.com/sports/polo (accessed May 17, 2019).

Lee, Jaeah, and Maya Dusenbery. "Charts: The State of Women's Athletics, 40 Years after Title IX." *Mother Jones*, June 22, 2012. https://www.motherjones.com/politics/2012/06/charts-womens-athletics-title-nine-ncaa/ (accessed February 13, 2019).

Lent, Cassidy. "No Minor Achievement." National Baseball Hall of Fame, n.d. https://baseballhall.org/discover/short-stops/ila-borders (accessed March 8, 2019).

Little, Becky. "The Most Controversial Census Changes in American History." History Channel, March 29, 2018. https://www.history.com/news/census-changes-controversy-citizenship (accessed May 26, 2019).

"LPGA Teaching and Club Professionals: A History," LPGA, n.d. http://www.lpga.com/tcp/historytcp (accessed February 5, 2019).

Mandell, Nina. "WNBA Players Respond to Ex-Player's Claims That 98 Percent of the League Is Gay." *USA Today*, February 22, 2017. https://www.usatoday.com/story/sports/ftw/2017/02/22/a-former-wnba-player-said-she-was-bullied-in-a-league-filled-with-jealousy-heres-how-wnba-players-responded/98242446/ (accessed March 31, 2019).

"The Mann Act." Public Broadcasting Service, n.d. https://www.pbs.org/kenburns/unforgivable-blackness/mann-act (accessed May 26, 2019).

Mannix, Chris. "High Hopes: He's Three Inches Taller Than Yao Ming, but Is Pro Hoops' Biggest Player Ready for the NBA?" *Sports Illustrated*, February 12, 2007. https://www.si.com/vault/2007/02/12/8400340/high-hopes (accessed February 17, 2019).

Marcin, Ashley. "The Average Heights of Men around the World." Healthline, n.d. https://www.healthline.com/health/average-height-for-men (accessed February 21, 2019).

Martin, Karin A. "Becoming a Gendered Body: Practices of Preschools." *American Sociological Review* 63, no. 4 (1998): 494–511.

Matthews, Melissa. "Women Are Better Athletes Than Men, Study about Gender Fitness Says." *Newsweek*, December 16, 2017. https://www.newsweek.com/women-are-better-athletes-men-study-about-gender-fitness-says-736047 (accessed March 6, 2019).

McCaul, Kevin D., Brian A. Gladue, and Margaret Joppa. "Winning, Losing, Mood, and Testosterone." *Hormone and Behavior* 26, no. 4 (1992): 486–504.

"Mission and History." Women's Football Alliance, n.d. http://www.wfaprofootball.com/about/ (accessed March 8, 2019).

Murchison, Gabe. *Supporting and Caring for Transgender Children*. Human Rights Campaign, September 2016. https://assets2.hrc.org/files/documents/SupportingCaringforTransChildren.pdf?_ga=2.132362249.647985918.1552655593-1879478770.1552655593 (accessed March 15, 2019).

Nauright, John. "Rugby." *Encyclopaedia Britannica*, n.d. https://www.britannica.com/sports/rugby (accessed July 9, 2019).

NCAA Office of Inclusion. *NCAA Inclusion of Transgender Athletes*. NCAA, 2011. http://www.ncaa.org/sites/default/files/Transgender_Handbook_2011_Final.pdf (accessed March 14, 2019).

"NFL Announces Five 2019 International Games." NFL.com, January 21, 2019. http://www.nfl.com/news/story/0ap3000001012392/article/nfl-announces-five-2019-international-games (accessed May 22, 2019).

"NFL Expands Rooney Rule Requirements to Strengthen Diversity." NFL.com, December 12, 2018. http://www.nfl.com/news/story/0ap3000000999110/article/nfl-expands-rooney-rule-requirements-to-strengthen-diversity (accessed May 30, 2019).

Niiler, Eric. "Testosterone Ruling for Athletes Fuels Debate over 'Natural' Ability." Wired, May 1, 2018. https://www.wired.com/story/testosterone-ruling-for-athletes-fuels-debate-over-natural-ability/ (accessed February 18, 2019).

Ninan, Susan. "Dutee Chand: I Have Found Life and Can Run without Fear Now." ESPN, April 28, 2018. http://www.espn.com/athletics/story/_/id/23336583/dutee-chand-found-life-run-fear-now (accessed February 18, 2019).

Nodkarni, Rohan, and Alex Nieves. "Why Missouri's Football Team Joined a Protest against School Administration." *Sports Illustrated*, November 9, 2015. https://www.si.com/college-football/2015/11/09/missouri-football-protest-racism-tim-wolfe (accessed June 6, 2019).

O'Callaghan, Eion. "Adam Rippon, John Curry, and Figure Skating's Complex History with Gay Athletes." *Guardian*, February 17, 2018. https://www.theguardian.com/sport/2018/feb/17/adam-rippon-lgbt-figure-skaters-john-curry (accessed May 9, 2018).

"Odds of a High School Female Athlete Going Pro." ScholarshipStats.com, n.d. http://www.scholarshipstats.com/odds-of-going-pro-women.htm (accessed July 12, 2019).

"On the Shoulders of Giants." National Public Radio, February 14, 2019. https://www.npr.org/templates/transcript/transcript.php?storyId=693878396 (accessed June 4, 2019).

O'Neal, Lonnae. "The Struggle Is Real: The Unrelenting Weight of Being a Black, Female Athlete." *The Undefeated*, June 25, 2018. https://theundefeated.com/features/the-struggle-is-real-the-unrelenting-weight-of-being-a-black-female-athlete/ (accessed July 7, 2019).

Padawer, Ruth. "The Humiliating Practice of Sex-Testing Female Athletes." *New York Times Magazine*, June 28, 2016. https://www.nytimes.com/2016/07/03/magazine/the-humiliating-practice-of-sex-testing-female-athletes.html (accessed July 16, 2019).

Page, Jason. "Opinion: Why Michael Sam Is a Footnote in History, Not a Trailblazer." NBCNews, August 23, 2016. https://www.nbcnews.com/feature/nbc-out/opinion-why-michael-sam-footnote-history-not-trailblazer-n634786 (accessed May 8, 2019).

Pearl, Diana. "Meet the First Woman to Earn an NCAA Football Scholarship." *People*, April 14, 2017. https://people.com/sports/meet-the-first-woman-to-earn-an-ncaa-football-scholarship/ (accessed March 8, 2019).

"RACE: The Power of an Illusion: The Difference between Us." California Newsreel, 2003. http://newsreel.org/video/race-the-power-of-an-illusion (accessed May 26, 2019).

Reed, Adam. "NBA Steps Up Its Global Plans to Take Basketball to New Markets." CNBC, January 18, 2019. https://www.cnbc.com/2019/01/18/nba-steps-up-its-global-plans-to-take-basketball-to-new-markets.html (accessed May 22, 2019).

Reed, David. "High Tributes Paid to Murphy." *Lexington Herald*, May 5, 1967. http://www.uky.edu/Projects/AfricanCem/reference/ref003002.html (accessed May 24, 2019).

Reid, Jason, and Jane McManus. "The NFL's Racial Divide." *The Undefeated*, n.d., https://theundefeated.com/features/the-nfls-racial-divide/ (accessed May 28, 2019).

"Report: MLB Revenues Exceed $10 Billion for the First Time." *USA Today*, November 22, 2017. https://www.usatoday.com/story/sports/mlb/2017/11/22/mlb-revenues-exceed-10-billion/890041001/ (accessed June 5, 2019).

"Reserve Clause." Baseball Reference, n.d. https://www.baseball-reference.com/bullpen/Reserve_clause (accessed June 5, 2019).

Rhoden, William C. "Major League Baseball Struck Out at the World Series by Not Facing Up to Blatant Racism." *The Undefeated*, November 2, 2017. https://theundefeated.com/features/major-league-baseball-struck-out-at-the-world-series-by-not-facing-up-to-blatant-racism/ (accessed June 7, 2019).

Roberts, M. B. "Rudolph Ran and World Went Wild." *ESPN*, n.d. https://www.espn.com/sportscentury/features/00016444.html (accessed June 4, 2019).

Ronnestad, Bent R., Havard Nyaard, and Truls Raastad. "Physiological Elevation of Endogenous Hormones Result in Superior Strength and Training Adaptation." *European Journal of Applied Physiology and Occupational Physiology* 111, no. 9 (2011): 2249–59.

Sabo, Don, and Philip Veliz. "Surveying Youth Sports in America: What We Do Know and What It Means for Public Policy." In *Child's Play: Sport in Kids' Worlds*, edited by Michael Messner and Michael Musto, 23–42. Rutgers, NJ: Rutgers University Press, 2016.

Saffer, Max. "Dollars but No Sense: Golf's Long History of Shortchanging Women." ESPNW, April 8, 2016. http://www.espn.com/espnw/sports/article/15160220/big-gap-earnings-men-women-professional-golfers (accessed March 7, 2019).

Said, Nick. "Meet France's World Cup Players with Deep African Roots." *Sunday Times*, July 1, 2018. https://www.timeslive.co.za/sport/soccer/2018-07-01-meet-frances-world-cup-players-with-deep-african-roots/ (accessed May 21, 2019).

Sanders, Alice. "Is Gender Segregation in Sports Necessary?" *How We Got to Now* (blog), July 29, 2016. http://www.pbs.org/how-we-got-to-now/blogs/howwegottonext/is-gender-segregation-in-sports-necessary/ (accessed March 6, 2019).

Savin-Williams, Ritch C. "A Guide to Genderqueer, Non-Binary, and Genderfluid Identity." *Psychology Today*, July 29, 2018. https://www.psychologytoday.com/us/blog/sex-sexuality-

and-romance/201807/guide-genderqueer-non-binary-and-genderfluid-identity (accessed July 6, 2019).

Schilt, Kristen, and Laurel Westbrook. "Bathroom Battlegrounds and Penis Panics." *Contexts*, August 20, 2015. https://contexts.org/articles/bathroom-battlegrounds-and-penis-panics/ (accessed March 18, 2019).

Schrack-Walters, Andrew, Kathleen O'Donnell, and Daniel L. Wadlow. "Deconstructing the Myth of the Monolithic Male Athlete: A Qualitative Study of Men's Participation in Athletics." *Sex Roles* 60, no. 1–2 (2009): 81–99.

Schrotenboer, Brent. "How NFL Owners Trip over Themselves Despite Wealth, Power." *USA Today*, March 28, 2019. https://www.usatoday.com/story/sports/nfl/2019/03/28/nfl-owners-wealth-cant-keep-them-out-trouble/3281774002/ (accessed May 30, 2019).

Schultz, Jaime. *Qualifying Times: Points of Change in U.S. Women's Sport*. Urbana: University of Illinois Press, 2014.

Schwartz, Larry. "Billie Jean Won for All Women." ESPN, n.d. https://www.espn.com/sportscentury/features/00016060.html (accessed June 5, 2019).

Schwartz, Larry. "Didrikson Was a Woman ahead of Her Time." ESPN, n.d. https://www.espn.com/sportscentury/features/00014147.html (accessed March 27, 2019).

Segal, Fred. "Wes Welker Was a Wayne Chrebet Type Who Was a Steve Trasker Type Who Was a Steve Largent Type." Freezing Cold Takes, January 31, 2017. http://thecomeback.com/freezingcoldtakes/nfl/wes-welker-wayne-chrebet-type-steve-tasker-type-steve-largent-type.html (accessed May 29, 2019).

Semuels, Alana. "Poor Girls Are Leaving Their Brothers Behind." *The Atlantic*, November 27, 2017. https://www.theatlantic.com/business/archive/2017/11/gender-education-gap/546677/ (accessed February 13, 2019).

Shadel, Jon. "This Gender Neutral Athlete Wants to End Sex Segregation in Sports." VICE, November 10, 2016. https://www.vice.com/en_us/article/mvk33x/this-gender-neutral-athlete-wants-to-end-sex-segregation-in-sports (accessed March 12, 2019).

Sheldon, Jane P., Toby Epstein Jayaratne, and Elizabeth M. Petty. "White Americans' Genetic Explanations for a Perceived Race Difference in Athleticism: The Relation to Prejudice toward and Stereotyping of Blacks." *Athletic Insight: The Online Journal of Sport Psychology* 9, no. 3 (2007): 31–56.

Sherman, Elizabeth. "Why Don't More People Consider Cheerleading a Sport?" *The Atlantic*, May 2, 2017. https://www.theatlantic.com/entertainment/archive/2017/05/why-dont-more-people-consider-competitive-cheerleading-a-sport/524940/ (accessed February 5, 2019).

Silverstein, Jason. "I Don't Feel Your Pain: A Failure of Empathy Perpetuates Racial Disparities." *Slate*, June 27, 2013. https://slate.com/technology/2013/06/racial-empathy-gap-people-dont-perceive-pain-in-other-races.html (accessed May 31, 2019).

Simpson, Jake. "How Title IX Sneakily Revolutionized Women's Sports." *The Atlantic*, June 21, 2012. https://www.theatlantic.com/entertainment/archive/2012/06/how-title-ix-sneakily-revolutionized-womens-sports/258708/ (accessed February 13, 2019).

Smith, Harrison. "Rene Portland, Penn State Basketball Coach Accused of Anti-Gay Discrimination, Dies at 65." *Washington Post*, July 23, 2018. https://www.washingtonpost.com/local/obituaries/rene-portland-penn-state-basketball-coach-accused-of-anti-gay-discrimination-dies-at-65/2018/07/23/625993d4-8e81-11e8-8322-b5482bf5e0f5_story.html?utm_term=.be1e7bb1b20b (accessed March 30, 2019).

Smith, Patrick. "Soccer in the Spotlight as Europe Grapples with Racism on and off the Field." NBCNews, April 14, 2019. https://www.nbcnews.com/news/world/soccer-spotlight-europe-grapples-racism-field-n992911 (accessed May 21, 2019).

Sonoma, Serena. "Black Trans Women Want the Media to Show Them Living, Not Just Dying." *Vox*, June 18, 2019. https://www.vox.com/first-person/2019/6/18/18679295/black-trans-women-murder-violence (accessed July 6, 2019).

Sotto, Michael. "Jason Collins' Coming Out Story: The Conversations, Emotions and Legacy behind His Comeback with the Nets." *The Athletic*, February 28, 2019. https://theathletic.com/841269/2019/02/28/jason-collins-coming-out-story-the-conversations-emotions-and-legacy-behind-his-comeback-with-the-nets/ (accessed March 25, 2019).

Sparhawk, Ruth M., Mary E. Leslie, Phyllis Y. Turbow, and Zina R. Rose. *American Women in Sport, 1887–1987: A 100-Year Chronology*. Metuchen, NJ: Scarecrow, 1989.

Starnes, DeAngelo. "The Lost History of Black Jockeys." *American Renaissance*, June 5, 2009. https://www.amren.com/news/2009/06/the_lost_histor/ (accessed May 24, 2019).

Stelle, Lauren. "Chris Mosier on Making History as First Trans Member of Team USA." *Rolling Stone*, August 2, 2016. https://www.rollingstone.com/culture/culture-sports/chris-mosier-on-making-history-as-first-trans-member-of-team-usa-250971/ (accessed May 6, 2019).

Stoddart, Brian. "Sport, Cultural Imperialism, and the Colonial Response in the British Empire." *Comparative Studies in Society and History* 30, no. 4 (1988): 649–73.

Storer, Thomas W., Lynne Magliano, Linda Woodhouse, Martin L. Lee, Connie Dzekov, Jeanne Dzekov, Richard Casaburi, and Shalender Bhasin. "Testosterone Dose-Dependently Increases Maximal Voluntary Strength and Leg Power, but Does Not Affect Fatigability of Specific Tension." *Journal of Clinical Endocrinology and Metabolism* 88, no. 4 (2003): 1478–85.

Strashin, Jamie. "What's the Real Problem with Caster Semenya?" CBC, May 14, 2018. https://www.cbc.ca/sports/olympics/trackandfield/caster-semenya-cultural-bias-1.4661929 (accessed July 5, 2019).

"Tallest Man Living." Guinness World Records, n.d. http://www.guinnessworldrecords.com/world-records/tallest-man-living (accessed February 22, 2019).

"Teams." Gay Football Supporters Network, n.d. https://www.gfsn.co.uk/?page_id=614 (accessed May 13, 2019).

theSCOREX. "NFL Census 2017–18." Medium, July 26, 2018. https://medium.com/thescorex/nfl-census-2017-18-34223d0148a7 (accessed July 18, 2019).

Thibault, Valerie, Marion Guillaume, Geoffroy Berthelot, Nour El Helou, Karine Schaal, Laurent Quinquis, Hala Nassif, Muriel Tafflet, Silvie Escolano, Olivier Hermine, and Jean-François Toussaint. "Women and Men in Sport Performance: The Gap Has Not Evolved Since 1983." *Journal of Sports Science and Medicine* 9, no. 2 (2010): 214–23.

Thorpe, J. R. "The Feminist History of Bicycles." *Bustle*, May 12, 2017. https://www.bustle.com/p/the-feminist-history-of-bicycles-57455 (accessed June 3, 2019).

"Top 10 Tallest Women in the World Right Now." JustRichest, n.d. https://justrichest.com/tallest-women-world/ (accessed February 22, 2019).

Tower, Nikole. "In an Ethnic Breakdown of Sports, NBA Takes Lead for Most Diverse." GlobalSportMatters, n.d. https://globalsportmatters.com/culture/2018/12/12/in-an-ethnic-breakdown-of-sports-nba-takes-lead-for-most-diverse/ (accessed May 29, 2019).

"Trans Athletes Make Great Gains, Yet Resentment Still Flares." NBCNews, February 25, 2019. https://www.nbcnews.com/feature/nbc-out/trans-athletes-make-great-gains-yet-resentment-still-flares-n975646 (accessed March 14, 2019).

"Turner Syndrome." Intersex Society of North America, n.d. http://www.isna.org/faq/conditions/turner (accessed February 8, 2019).

"Unapologetic: The Black Female Athlete." *The Undefeated*, February 24, 2018. https://theundefeated.com/videos/unapologetic-the-black-female-athlete-2/ (accessed July 12, 2019).

Vines, Gail. "Last Olympics for the Sex Test?" NewScientist, July 4, 1992. https://www.newscientist.com/article/mg13518284-900-last-olympics-for-the-sex-test/ (accessed February 17, 2019).

Volz, B. D. "Race and Quarterback Survival in the National Football League." *Journal of Sports Economics* 18, no. 8 (2017): 850–66.

Wade, Lisa. "The New Science of Sex Difference." *Sociology Compass* 7, no. 4 (2013): 278–93.

Wade, Lisa. "When Jews Dominated Professional Basketball." Sociological Images, November 25, 2013. https://thesocietypages.org/socimages/2013/11/25/when-jews-dominated-professional-basketball/ (accessed May 29, 2019).

Waldner, L. K., A. Sikka, and S. Baig. "Ethnicity and Sex Differences in University Student's Knowledge of AIDS, Fear of AIDS, and Attitudes toward Gay Men." *Journal of Homosexuality* 37, no. 3 (1999): 117–33.

Ward, E. G. "Homophobia, Hypermasculinity and the U.S. Black Church." *Culture, Health and Sexuality* 7, no. 5 (2007): 493–504.

Washington, Jesse. "Still No Anthem, Still No Regrets for Mahmoud Abdul-Raud." *The Undefeated*, September 1, 2016. https://theundefeated.com/features/abdul-rauf-doesnt-regret-sitting-out-national-anthem/ (accessed June 7, 2019).

Washington, Robert E., and David Karen. "Sport and Society." *Annual Review of Sociology* 27 (2001): 187–212.

Weisberg, Lori. "Is Owning a Baseball Team a Money Maker?" *San Diego Union Tribune*, August 7, 2012. https://www.sandiegouniontribune.com/sports/padres/sdut-owning-a-baseball-team-rarely-a-losing-proposition-2012aug07-story.html (accessed June 5, 2019).

Willis, Teresa. "Kicking Down Barriers: Gay Footballers, Challenging Stereotypes, and Changing Attitudes in Amateur League Play." *Soccer & Society* 16, no. 2–3 (2014): 377–92.

Wilson, Julee. "Haters Attack Gabby Douglas' Hair Again and Twitter Promptly Claps Back." *Essence*, August 8, 2016. https://www.essence.com/news/gabby-douglas-hair-haters-twitter-claps-back/ (accessed July 12, 2019).

Winslow, Barbara. "The Impact of Title IX." *History Now: The Journal of the Gilder Lehrman Institute of American History*, September 24, 2016. https://faculty.uml.edu/sgallagher/The_Impact_of_Title_IX-_GilderLehrman.pdf (accessed February 13, 2019).

Withycombe, Jenny Lind. "Intersecting Selves: African American Female Athletes Experiences of Sport." *Sociology of Sport Journal* 28 (2011): 478–93.

"Woman Kicks Extra Points." *New York Times*, October 20, 1997. https://www.nytimes.com/1997/10/20/sports/woman-kicks-extra-points.html (accessed February 13, 2019).

Wong, Curtis M. "Michael Sam Says He's Been Told He's Not Gay or Black Enough." *Huffpost*, March 31, 2016. https://www.huffpost.com/entry/michael-sam-racism-gay-community_n_56fd38a6e4b0daf53aeee64e (accessed May 10, 2019).

Wright, Branson. "The Only MLB All-Star Game That Featured Two African-American Starting Pitchers." *The Undefeated*, July 9, 2019. https://theundefeated.com/features/the-only-mlb-all-star-game-that-featured-two-african-american-starting-pitchers/ (accessed July 11, 2019).

"Yoshida Has RBI Single in First At-Bat." *ESPN*, May 30, 2010. http://www.espn.com/minorlbb/news/story?id=5233233 (accessed March 8, 2019).

Young, Iris Marion. *Throwing Like a Girl and Other Essays in Feminist Philosophy and Social Theory*. Bloomington: Indiana University Press, 1990.

Zeigler, Cyd. *Fair Play: How LGBT Athletes Are Claiming Their Rightful Place in Sports*. Brooklyn, NY: Akashic Books, 2016.

Zieralski, Ed. "Timeline: Horse Racing's Women Jockeys." *San Diego Union-Tribune*, June 8, 2013. https://www.sandiegouniontribune.com/sports/horse-racing/sdut-women-jockeys-horse-racing-2013jun08-htmlstory.html (accessed February 5, 2019).

Zirin, Dave. *A People's History of Sports in the United States: 250 Years of Politics, Protest, People and Play*. New York: New Press, 2008.

Zirin, Dave. "Nick Bosa and the NFL's Double Standards." *Edge of Sports*, April 27, 2019. https://www.edgeofsports.com/2019-04-27-1432/index.html (accessed June 7, 2019).

INDEX

ABOUT THE AUTHOR

Robyn Ryle is a writer, sociologist, professor of gender studies, and lover of sports. She has been teaching classes about gender, race, and sport at Hanover College, in Hanover, Indiana, for 15 years. Ryle has written a sociology of gender textbook, *Questioning Gender: A Sociological Exploration*, now in its fourth edition. *She/He/They/Me: For the Sisters, Misters and Binary Resisters* is her nonfiction book about gender told in the style of a choose-your-own-adventure. She attended Millsaps College in Jackson, Mississippi, for her undergraduate degree and Indiana University, Bloomington for her PhD. She lives in Madison, Indiana, in a 180-year-old house with her husband, daughter, and two cats.